One of Seven

A Survivor's True Story of Molestation and Healing

By: Olivia Ivons-Bosco

ISBN-10: 1453706658
EAN-13: 9781453706657
Library of Congress Control Number: 2010911520

This book is dedicated to my husband.
Thank you for being my hero, knight in shining armor,
my best friend,
and for loving me just as I am.

My daughters, thank you for being my inspiration
to live and spread my wings.

And to Janet, thanks for being open and helping me see past
the black clouds so I could continue achieving my goals.

Table of Contents

Introduction

Words of wisdom and little sayings have always been sort of a pastime for me. I grew up with my mother and grandmother speaking them often. One that stands out in my mind is "Feed the birds and never go hungry." As I grew in age, I would read or hear a quote and be impressed by how deeply it made me think. "Destiny is what you do with your fate." Give it some thought. Think long enough, and your mind could take you hundreds of miles away. I think about this short line daily. It's become my life's motto in many ways.

Often I find myself browsing through shops I discover along my path. Not just to buy that item that screams, *Take me home*, but to also be inspired in some way. At times, an object sitting on a shelf with many other items will jump out and remind me of a good memory or a person I know. Colors and textures pop out too. I assume it's my own form of color therapy. Better yet for my wallet's sake, looking is free.

The other things I seek out in these quaint shops are small wooden plaques with simple verses. I'll read one, and my mind will ponder over it. Realizing how it relates to my life, or me I crave that click and the sudden *Wow!* or *Aha!*

This past summer, it seemed every other store I went into had merchandise saying: "Everyone's story begins at home." So truthful and realistic, it would be almost impossible for anyone to deny. I certainly can't.

No two of us have the same story. Yet they all create who we are and what we become, further proving that destiny does come from what you do with your fate. Coincidentally, others' stories can have an effect on a listener's destiny. In the same aspect, hearing about another's life can be a rare moment of fate that can change someone else's life for better or worse. It all depends on the outcome and how the story-holder dealt with their fate.

There is a lot I'd like to share about my beginning at home because I know there are others out there who have similar beginnings. I was molested for years by a few of my older brothers—my traumatic fate that led me to what I was destined. Perhaps my story will be the moment of fate that causes someone to gain absolution and peace within themselves. If not that, then I hope at least the knowledge they are not alone in their past history can give them a glimmer of hope that their story could have a happy ending.

I believe it is my destiny, caused by my own fate, to put my personal and private story in ink. My heart aches for those who have never been able to resolve their inner torment and for those who cannot achieve an inner balance to at least accept and try to move on. It's important to seek understanding, and for some it becomes an obsession. Most who do find it get there by reaching out for professional help in a variety of ways. Oddly, I took a different route, but I have traveled a long way from my original home life. No matter which way we seek answers to our start, we have to overcome obstacles and cling to the small achievements we make along the way to survive and continue forward. Today, I am at peace with my beginnings and wish the same for anyone who has not yet reached their desire of the same.

CHAPTER I

Summing Me Up in a Nutshell

And so, my story begins at home.

My parents raised us all in the three-bedroom home that my father built himself. Our little hometown was just minutes away from Philadelphia. I am one of seven children. My sister and I are the only girls. We have five brothers.

Having so many children nowadays is rare, although not an odd thing for a committed Catholic family of my generation or of our community. Actually, we were of average size. There were families of a dozen and more near us.

My mother kept us all in line. It was daily routine for her to spit-shine our faces with her thumb and own saliva as we lined up to head out to school. The same routine was followed when leaving for church, grocery shopping, or a family picnic.

Having so many children and being a homemaker, you can imagine the workload on my mother each day. Our relationship back then could best be described as one of nourishing with little to no nurturing. Getting us fed, dressed, and educated, in the school sense, were so time-consuming, it left little time for her to nurture us, hug and kiss us, have one-on-one time, positively reinforce us, or even encourage us to live our dreams.

My father worked a swing shift, plus overtime, at the local steel mill and earned extra income through a small cement business in our backyard. Clearly, if he was not working to provide for us, he was catching what little sleep he could. Ironically, he found the time with my mom to make a family of seven.

I am number six in the line of siblings. My one sister is nine years older than I. She was sort of a mother-type figure growing up due to the age span. Today, even though there is a generation gap between us and we have opposite personalities, we have our own unique bond as sisters.

I have four older brothers and one who is younger. I feared all my brothers as a kid because of the pranks brothers in general tend to play. For far more extreme reasons, I feared Brothers Number One, Two, and Three. They were my molesters. Although it may be hard to comprehend, I did not fully hate them. I hated what they repeatedly did to me. Even at a young age, I somehow knew to differentiate the emotion. Now, I am not close to any of my five brothers. Not because of the past, but basically, we have little in common. We are all on different levels.

My preteen and teen years were horrendous. Typical peer pressure is enough for a young person to handle, but mine had the added issues of molestation and incest, resulting in fear and trust issues. I made very few friends and never had an adult mentor, who I could have benefited from greatly. School studies were beyond frazzling to me. Consumed by deep-seated emotions and ideas that come from such a trauma, I could hardly concentrate on much else. Many days I just wanted to give up. Luckily, I was blessed with a good sense of intuition. Somehow, that kept telling me there was more out there and a better life was out there too. I just had to hang on.

The better did come, and the wait was well worth it. I met someone who loves me for me unconditionally. I never once thought I was deserving of this type or any other type of love.

So naturally, when it hit me like a lead balloon, I was stunned. But I was smart enough to grab a hold of it and grow with it. Before I knew it, I was finding I was capable of returning the same type of love. Even though I was a little unsure of myself, I didn't doubt his words or actions for a second. He fully had my trust.

Completely going against tradition of long dating periods, we were talking marriage and setting plans into action after a few months. We married two years later in 1986. He was and still is the love of my life.

It took me a long period of time to be sure it wasn't a dream or that it all would be taken away from me. At this point, I still wasn't sure of why I deserved such a special person in my life.

Twenty-plus years later, I still have the same love as I did on day one. He remains my hero and my equal partner. He made me believe fairy tales can happen in the present day. He has helped me cope through many stages of my acceptance of and recovery from the past.

Finally, for the first time ever, I gained a best friend. He truly is my "BFF." He has been there through the roughest, as well as the best, times of my life.

With him, I became a parent in 1988. Together we have two beautiful, smart, outgoing, independent, and unique daughters. They are the best any parent could wish for.

Many of the steps I took toward recovery were not only to better myself, but also to enable me to be a more stable-minded mother to my children. I wanted to nourish and nurture them. Another one of my life's mottos is: "Count your blessings, not your problems." I certainly count both my daughters as blessings.

As far as a career, I can't say I have one. I won't beat around the bush as to why I haven't taken one or the other direction yet. It's quite simple. I haven't decided what I want to be when I fully grow up yet. Then there are the more obvious reasons, such as financing for schooling, lack of self-worth, fear of change, and no support or encouragement. You know, all those minute reasons that we all consider when making choices in life. And truthfully, I couldn't focus even if all those reasons hadn't been in the way. I was so consumed on seeking resolution as to why I deserved to be molested as a child, I wouldn't have lived up to my full potential and would have done half jobs. I needed to have answers for all questions. Without them, I was stalled in developing into me and who I am.

I have had many jobs through the years. Many of these were to keep a penny in my pocket and for social interaction away from the daily routine at home. Working supplied the break from motherhood that was needed while my girls still needed me every day. Once again, I am the minority in statistics. Both parents work in a high percentage of households. I had the advantage of my husband making enough to make ends meet. He also didn't mind if I stayed home. He understood

I was on a search for my pot of gold, on a very personal level, at the end of a severely clouded rainbow.

Fully recovered, I still have not decided on a specific field or title. I have my ideas, but some college education is needed. On my list of things to accomplish, school is within grasp and a highly possible reality in the near future. I do know my dream job will be one where I work with my hands, mental thought, and my imagination and will involve some type of service to others.

Volunteering was another way to keep busy. School and neighborhood committees and church functions were all on my agenda. You name it, I did it. Volunteering became almost like an addiction to me. Easily, I could put in forty to sixty hours a week working on projects. The most rewarding and longest volunteer service I provided was for a nonprofit organization for young girls. I spent fifteen years mentoring girls to become strong, independent, and responsible adults. To have just one girl come back, and to hear her say that you made a difference to her, is the greatest compliment one can ever receive.

I began volunteering very shortly after I had all the answers except one regarding being molested. With most of my search done, I only had left to ask: what do I do now, and where do I go next? Things about me were changing, and much already had. Realizing this, the fear of change set in. I have the horrible habit of not taking opportunities when they are at my feet. I avoided the question. However, change is inevitable. The sooner anyone accepts this, the better they will be. For numerous years I sank deep into volunteering, making others feel better about themselves, but I avoided my own self. Resistance wasn't possible anymore. All the volunteer time began to wear on me, physically and mentally. I was being taken for granted almost to the point of abuse. All the negative feelings I had as a kid and young adult were starting to return. It wasn't until I completely broke down from it that I realized I needed to work on what I needed. It all summed up to that one question. What do I do now that I have all my questions? Things had to change. I had to face the fact that, with all the answers, I couldn't linger in the shell of the poor little molested girl anymore. She had more knowledge and couldn't pass yet another opportunity to grow.

I learned to say no and don't volunteer anymore. Instead I spend my free time for me. I devote time to my hobbies, which include crochet, painting, crafting, sewing, and baking. I've put many an hour into decorating my home and clearing all the clutter so that it is more peaceful and relaxing for all of us. I also love to surf the Net. I feed my constant need for new knowledge.

In the search for my final answer, I became interested in the metaphysical. Some things that started as a pastime and technique to combat stress and anxiety have become favorite diversions. Some have become daily parts of my life. Meditation and crystal therapy have benefited me immensely. You can often find me working with my crystal pendulums also. When not dowsing with one, I am custom-making them to sell to family, friends, and word-of-mouth customers. I am aware there are many people out there who would criticize these activities and more. The unopen critic will tell you they don't work or it's all gibberish. Everyone is entitled to his or her opinion. It happens to work for me. Moreover, my opinion is, if holding a rock (crystal) makes you feel better about yourself, another, or a situation you are in, then hold a rock. By far, it is much cheaper than paying for a psychiatrist and medications.

I do not currently have a real busy social life. I attended astrology classes every Monday night for several years. It was rare for me to miss a class. Once again, not everyone believes in it, and I can say I was a tad skeptical of it at first. What I learned was rather interesting and practical. Through this extensive study of the horoscope, I've learned to accept not only myself but others for their positive points and their shortcomings.

Another benefit of studying astrology is the opportunity to help others see why they may be struggling through different scenarios. Nowadays I use the skills I learned to read family and acquaintances charts. Looking at their natal, along with their progressed, chart will often show signs that these situations can occur at the exact time they are really happening. When I explain what the signs and planets in the houses signify, it's amazing to see people's expressions when the head of the nail is being hit dead-on. It makes it easier for them to accept themselves, and their issue at hand, and persevere through.

My goals in life right now are to express my self-confidence more often and to finish raising my daughters (like that will ever end). Next in line would be, as I mentioned before, taking some college courses. My list also includes finding free time for my husband from his demanding job and finding more free time alone, to go on a date now and again (of course with each other), and to complete what I believe is my last step of recovery, to give back.

Beyond that, my plans are to strive to be a more loving and better person each day. Basically, continue "growing up." I use the word "continue" because, are any of us ever done?

I am a survivor, just like many others in the world. Perhaps, I am further along in my survival. If you happen to be a victim also, the fact is, by breathing and reading this, you are surviving also. As long as we reach for help or continue to have hope, we are survivors by that alone. I find it rather ironic how you get the title of survivor after you've resolved all your issues with it. I think you earn that title the minute the horrible deed being done to you ceases. To get up or out and move on rather than lie there and die is survival. Whether it's an hour, a month, fifty years later, or you take it to the grave, you still faced each day, lived with the act and the aftereffects, dealt with them or kept them hidden. You still kept going. You survived.

If I had given up as a teen, I would be living in a shell of existence, a walking, breathing vegetable with a mind full of hatred, guilt, and fear. What feelings I'd have would be buried so deep inside a living casket that nothing would surface, making me completely numb. I would not have my best friend and spouse, my children, my new friends, or a positive story to tell. I think of all the birthdays, holidays, school plays, award ceremonies, and pieces of refrigerator art I would have missed. I wouldn't be able to tell you that, for some unknown purpose, being molested happened to me.

I used to, but no longer keep asking, *What if?* What if I had different parents, friends, or a mentor that I could tell? What if I had not met my husband? What if I had different or no brothers? It does not matter about the what-ifs because I cannot go back and change the order of events. Just because I gained some self-confidence doesn't give me almighty powers. Besides, my intuition told me long ago that no matter how or why it happened, it did. Somehow no matter how terrible, it helped me to make shape of myself and become the "me" I am today. I would not have such a high standard of morals and be a stickler for them if I had given up eons ago. This further strengthens my belief that destiny is what you do with the fate dealt you.

I cannot tell you recovery, forgiveness, peace, or self-esteem comes overnight or in a few years' time. The time is different for everyone. We all process at different rates. On my own, from the time as a teen when I really began to suffer, until the day I sent a letter to my brothers, my molesters, it took about twelve years. Add the seventeen or so years since then it's taken me to discover myself and the need to reach out and share, and you see it has taken me a long time. When you see the number twenty-nine, you can translate that into a quarter-plus of a century. Every minute of it was worth it. For every fear I faced, I gained courage. For every answer I accepted, I gained knowledge. For every ounce of forgiveness I gave, I gained release. For every moment in a day, good or bad, I grew and continue growing as a survivor who is living the next quarter century of her life guilt-free and at peace experiencing life as it should be.

CHAPTER 2

Parental Ties

It's common sense to understand my siblings and I share the same parents. It's much harder to grasp this concept: my parents are also the parents of my molesters.

I struggled with this for many moons. It ate away at me that it was even possible. What happened? Did my mother do drugs when she was pregnant with my three oldest brothers? Was there something different in the water for pregnancy two, five, six, and seven?

Absolutely not! My mom never did drugs, never smoked cigarettes or any other substance. Other than an occasional highball or glass of wine, she was not an alcoholic either.

Maybe it was my father's fault. Not. Of course, he had his beer each day. It was the norm to stop by the local tavern after work and knock back a couple before heading home. With his swing-shift schedule, that meant biweekly he would be on his way home while the bar was open. A biweekly alcoholic, I doubted it.

As far as drugs go, never. I can't recall him even taking an aspirin for a headache, and neither can my siblings. Furthermore, he drank the same well water my mother did.

So, how could three out of seven children have this evilness in them to molest their younger sister? I don't know. In the process of recovering, I could only speculate and rationalize about this question and many others.

I am not a medical professional, and by far I am nowhere near being a scientist. After years of being haunted by my above question, I put together what I did know and what I didn't. The three had gotten something different. Perhaps they had gotten different genes when it came to our mental makeups.

After all, the seven of us were very similar in appearance physically, yet had our differences. Some shared features that one or two of us did not have. Three of us shared another physical trait that, however, the other four didn't show. Physically, anyone could see the similarities but at the same time see our individuality because of slight differences. We certainly were not cloned.

A lightbulb went off, well, my intuition, and I was able to put it into words and understand. What's inside all of us was similar, yet different also. Mentally, some of us shared the same qualities, while others shared different ones. I accepted this as my answer and moved on to the next issue that seemed to burden me.

I've noticed often in society, after hearing of the tragic story of a child being abused or victimized, we put a spotlight on the parental figures even after we know who the abuser was. Think of the common story of a babysitter physically abusing a child. Give it a brief amount of time, and we ask ourselves, *Where were the parents, and why didn't they know sooner?* Or if it's the story of a father molesting a child, eventually we ask about the whereabouts of the mother.

It's only natural to question the parental figures. As a society, we believe it's their job to be the ultimate protectors and never let anything unpleasant happen to their offspring. Human nature instills in us to feel the need to further blame, and often we forget to look further at the abuser.

I assume with confidence that others go through the same or similar thinking when they are personally the victim. Restating, I am not a medical professional, but without doubt this was the natural process for me. I further rationalized blaming my parents with the fact they didn't keep me from harm. I lost trust in them and their parenting.

I turned the spotlight on both my parents. I screamed the questions inside me: Where were they? And how did they allow this to happen?

They didn't allow it. It wasn't until my confrontation with my brothers became known that they found out. That was about fifteen years after the molesting stopped.

You also may be wondering where they were. In plain words, they were busy providing food and shelter for us. I felt resentment and disgust toward them the minute I began pondering their whereabouts.

I needed their undivided attention. All lights should have been shining on me. That was almost an impossibility with so many of us needing attention. Of course, if one of us was ill, we took center stage. It had to be visible to the eye, physically visible. My suffering and ailment weren't at the forefront and out in the open, therefore easily not seen at all.

My memory of my father while all of this was happening was that of an absent one. Not in the sense of abandonment, but in the sense of working every possible hour for financial reasons. He often worked overtime on special projects at the mill. It entailed working in excessive heat for eight to twelve-hour shifts. It's one thing to be tired, but add the exhaustion from the heat. No wonder it seemed like he slept most of the hours he was home.

Looking back to where my mom was, I see her doing tons of laundry. Even in the dead of winter, clothes and linens were hung outside from sunrise to sunset. She seemed to be cooking or preparing a meal simultaneously. Packing lunches was a daily assembly line. Baking was done on Sunday for the week. There was no break by ordering out for pizza. I was thirteen or fourteen before that became a time-saving option. Sewing and mending were a common occurrence, even at late hours of night. Mom loved her soap operas. I don't remember ever seeing her sit to watch them. They were more background noise as she cleaned house and made beds. In today's world, she'd be considered a queen of multitasking.

Other than my father taking my mother to the grocery store once a week, I can't think of a time they went out together and alone. Unless I count my grandfather's viewing and funeral when I was five. Dad would drop Mom off at the grocery and come back home to do yard chores or work in his cement area until she would call to let us know she was done shopping.

It was those times, which was most of the time, when both my parents were consumed by chores and work, that one of the three brothers would take advantage and prey on me. It was never all three at once and, luckily for me, never two taking their opportunities in one day.

I was always thankful for all my parents gave me, but it still felt like they were responsible for my dilemma. It didn't fully dawn on me that you can't be with your children 24-7 until I had my own children many years later.

When my oldest daughter was in first grade, she struggled with a few of the other girls in her class. As much as she complained about them picking on her, she tried again each day to befriend them in the schoolyard. I would encourage her to be herself, hold her chin up, and ignore them. What I really wanted to tell her was to wallop them right between the eyes. That wouldn't have been very motherly of me. Besides, I didn't want my daughter to be a bully either. Things calmed down and worked out for her given a little time. All along, I fought the urge to march into the school office and demand the teacher or principal do something about her wicked little foes.

I then understood no parent can watch over their children every moment of the day. No matter how hard you obsess, you cannot give your kids all they need or want materially or mentally. I applied the same thinking to my whole childhood and my relationship with my parents.

The resentment and anger toward my parents began to ease. It didn't dissolve instantly. Today, I can say they didn't deserve any of my blame for what my brothers did or for not seeing. They were naive to it. They were devoted to providing for a family, physically and financially struggling to give all of us the best upbringing and education possible.

(Do the math: seven kids times seven Catholic school tuitions times twelve years for each sums up to a whole hell of a lot of sacrifice and money.)

We were all cared for physically beyond the call of duty. Parenting lacked when it came to the mental sense. My rearing was off balance by a wide margin. But surely, people have been raised worse.

My outlook is my parents did the best they could. There is not one parent in this world who, on the day their first child was born, was supplied with a manual telling them how to raise a child evenly and perfectly.

In someone else's epic saga, maybe their parents were guilty and allowed treacherous things to happen for one or various reasons. Then I have to agree: these victims are entitled to their grudges and anger. By all means, though, try to work through it. If not for forgiveness, at least so the parents' faults are no longer taken on as your own. Every victim needs to know they themselves are not to blame. I was fortunate to rid my mind of this added complication early in the healing process. Every case of a childhood scarred has its own original twist and ending.

When questioning where my parents were, I even pointed the spot-light at my only sister. Why not? She shared the same bedroom, and in my mind, she should have been able to stop the abuse because she was the big sister.

Due to the age gap, she at times was more motherly than sisterly to me. But she wasn't my mother. For that reason, it wasn't her job to constantly watch over me.

While this was happening to me, my sister was out of the house. As a young teen, she'd be babysitting or sleeping over a friend's house at night. Later, when she was old enough, she'd be working or out with friends at the clubs until late. She was married at twenty and moved out altogether.

Boy, that was a struggle for me when she left. I was devastated. Even though I was molested while she was out, I still looked at her as protection. All those nights she was home and in her twin bed next to mine, I knew there was no chance one of my brothers could crawl past her to my bed.

I regret sending any blame her way. At the age of twenty-seven, I finally told her everything. So many things made sense to her. Certain behaviors I had growing up that were unexplainable suddenly fit the picture. My never wanting to sleep or even go to bed at night took on a whole new light for her. It wasn't the occasional nightmare she thought I struggled with. She took my behavior by day as being a plain old brat. Now she realized I was acting out for attention and lived in fear. I was a little girl trying to get noticed so my torment would end.

She felt guilty for not being there and apologized profusely. She only wished I could have put it into words and told her many years ago. She didn't think less of me, as I imagined anybody would if they knew the truth.

I never really thought to tell her. I had no idea that I could go to her. In the present day, we teach children to reach out to any adult they feel safe with. Back then, you only told a parent if absolutely necessary or bit your tongue forever. The other rule was no tattling. I didn't know there was a difference on telling for safety reasons and just tattling to be a busybody. Still, some things weren't told or discussed ever. I knew I should have gone in the confessional and told the parish priest, but then I would have gone to hell for my sins. I must have been daydreaming when they talked about being forgiven. Therefore, when I made my First Penance in second grade, and all the times after, I went into the secret box, knelt, and gave Father Whoever my laundry list of itty-bitty sins, said the Hail Mary prayer three times, and went home with my secret still untold.

Besides, my brothers each told me never to tell anyone or I'd be in trouble and something really bad would happen to me. I was small and gullible. I believed them. Cancer was still "the C-word." No adult even dared to speak the full word. Not a soul ever said what would happen to you if you did say the full word out loud, so it had to be bad. Imagine if a young girl had brought up a new subject and it was "the M-word": molestation.

Stop imagining. I can tell you firsthand. In a few words, it wasn't a pretty scene.

It was an average dinnertime setting. Most of us were around the table in our assigned seats.

My sister was out that evening. My dad was on middle shift, so wasn't home this particular evening. It was meatloaf night. The normal verbal bantering among siblings was being exchanged back and forth across the table.

You know how it goes. Kid Numer One says, "What are you looking at?"

Then Kid Number Two, looking Kid Number One square in the eye, sarcastically replies back, "I don't know, but it's pretty ugly-looking.

Kids Three to Six are laughing hysterically at them.

One needs to envision all of us crammed around the table.

Elbow space is not a luxury you get too often in a large family. Mom is busy serving up green beans, applesauce, and the meatloaf. Everyone is trying to reach for the Kool-Aid pitcher before someone takes too much and leaves everyone else with nothing.

Give it a minute, or two at the max, and you will hear, "Move your elbow."

"Well your knee is past the imaginary line on the bench."

If your space wasn't being invaded, you were giggling at the sitcom.

"Mom, he's touching me."

All was typical until the next line, spoken aloud for all to hear, came from me, Kid Number Six. "Oh yeah? Well, him, him, and him touched my pee-pee hole down there. Bet you didn't know that. Now try and top me."

Ka-blam! went mom's pot of veggies on the counter. Simultaneous were a few elongated "ew's" from the nonmolesters and "shut up's" from the molesters.

For a brief second I thought, *Thank God, it's out. Mom knows now. Those three are going to get the belt to them, and they will never touch me again.*

Mom spoke finally, and all my hope was shattered. She reprimanded me instead. "Okay. That is enough, young lady. Where did you learn such language? Do not ever let me hear you talk like that again. I'll wash your mouth out with soap."

It felt like a hundred daggers went into my heart or my mother had just ripped it out to use in tomorrow's stew. The lump in my throat was as big as the beat-up volleyball we kicked around out back. Courageously, I didn't let one tear squeeze out from behind my eyes. The agonizing, gut-wrenching feeling of defeat would stay with me into adulthood. I would never dare try to tell anyone again until I was nineteen and dating my husband.

Surely, all my siblings were giggling under their breath. I know they were thinking I had just pushed the limit with our mother too far and had gotten what I deserved. Without doubt, the three brothers who should have gotten at least the fiercest of tongue-lashings were having a field day in their minds at how things had just backfired on me. Relishing their prize, they were still in the clear with halos gleaming.

I just hung my head and stared at my plate. I didn't dare look at anyone else out of embarrassment and fear. I slowly took one small bite at a time. Gulping to get the food past the lump still in my throat and trying not to gag, I had to eat the food I no longer had an appetite for. Otherwise, I would have been punished for wasting good food. I made sure I was one of the last to leave the table that night. I left without saying a word, went straight to bed without putting on my pajamas, and cried myself to sleep. I gripped tight to the pillows over my head so no one would hear my sobs or gasp for air.

What innocence that wasn't taken from being molested was lost that evening. I lost trust in my mom. I was entitled, just like every other kid, to trust and believe in my mother. It simply vanished quicker than water into a sponge.

Admit it—I have. It was ungodly poor timing on my part for such an announcement. I knew what my brothers were doing to me was wrong because it just didn't seem right. Nor did it feel good. Concluding I had to tell on them was good on my part. It never entered my eight-year-old mind that where and when I told on them mattered.

My mother's reaction was not the expected. For that alone I cried enough tears over the decades to have a lake named after me. On the other hand, what came out of my mouth had caught my mom off guard completely. I didn't hate my mom for not jumping to my rescue that night. I had a disappointment that caused a drastic void in my heart.

This was the early seventies. You didn't speak of such subjects because you never heard of them. So, there was no reason to ever think it would be in your own home. It was this naivety that kept not just my mother, but my father also, blind to even the possibility of it happening right under their noses.

Once again, cancer wasn't cancer, but "the C-word." Even in midsentence, "the C-word" was lowered to a bare whisper. Television consisted of *The Brady Bunch* and *The Waltons*. The closing line was always: *"Good night, John Boy."* It was never: *"Good night, John Boy. Now don't dare sneak in your little sister's room to touch her and stick your penis where it doesn't belong."*

There were no daily talk shows discussing the taboos of the world. Nor were there guest psychologists explaining how someone could mentally break taboos, or offering advice how to help victims overcome their suffering.

No commercial displayed a hotline number at the end. The most serious ad, not even related to self-help, was a Keep America Beautiful commercial that had an Indian chief with a tear rolling down his face because the Americans had scattered trash all over his beloved land.

I myself began to see generational difference of then and now in the mid-eighties. All of a sudden, there were gay people in the world. It seemed like AIDS arriving in our country opened a lot of closets and windows too.

Suddenly there were talk shows on the tube. It was as if you went to bed one night and the next morning when you awoke all that was on TV anymore were these shows. Every talk show and news channel had pieces on things that happened behind closed doors. In addition, they featured therapists and psychiatrists giving their diagnoses, case scenarios, and theories right on screen. Wow. I became aware of this whole line of people one could go to like they were a parent. Only difference being, you paid them. If you were brave enough to go tell them, they would listen and help you. I didn't run for the phone and call one. Money was an obstacle, and bravery was definitely not in my self-description. Always in the back of my mind, I kept the notion that if I couldn't get through the turmoil and emotions caused by my childhood drama alone, I could fall back on one of these professional people. Just the idea gave me a sheer glimmer of hope.

A few months after I was married, I was home alone in our apartment. With a little spare time before starting dinner, I turned on the TV and decided to look at the *Oprah* show, which everyone was abuzz about. Her guests that day had all been molested by a family member, close relative, or someone they knew. I just sat bug-eyed at the screen, not even hearing the words being said although lips were moving. I knocked back into my seat, stunned, much like a ton of bricks had hit me and the little cartoon stars were revolving around my head.

I found out I wasn't the only person to ever be molested. For the first time, I was seeing other victims, and dear Lord, they were on national television. Having visuals to connect with what I only thought true in my mind was overwhelming as much as it was enlightening.

I suspected others somewhere suffered the same ordeal as me. Never having it proven otherwise, I doubted myself and took on the shame that molestation was of my own uniqueness. Often my mind and gut instinct contradicted one another. I battled a constant emotional seasickness until one, if not the other, bailed ship or I found proof and pushed it overboard. This combat within me came out as the daily physical feeling of constant nausea.

The people I saw on-screen stayed in my mind for months. Until I fully absorbed and analyzed my new knowledge, I thought about them every day. The final result was the feeling of some weight being lifted off my shoulders. I'll never meet or know who these people were, so

I can only express my gratitude here in ink. If it were not for their own tragedy, their own search for resolution, and their courage, I may not have reaped that little bit of hope. Thanks, for you made a difference to me.

I daydreamed very frequently as a child, a teen, and still do sometimes as an adult. It was an escape, my only escape at times. I'd put new details to old situations and replay them in my own little fantasy world. I didn't do it intentionally. It just happened that way. Similar to the repetitive what-if questions, this was like the virtual reality form, and the object was to uncover things you didn't view or understand before.

One day, replaying the scene of the infamous Meatloaf Night for about the thousandth time in my life, I waited until I was the last one at the table to talk to my mom. Earlier that day, she hadn't turned the television off after her soaps. Someone had stopped by to do the cooking for her. This gave her time to sit and watch one of the talk shows that now followed the soaps. Mom became aware, just like me, that this does happen more than people knew. She was also smarter from it and a little less naive. This time around, Mom reacted differently than she ever had before when I told her. My daydream ended with her sitting next to me, holding my hand.

Was my fantasizing some form of hypnotherapy? Beats me. Nor does it really matter whether it was or wasn't. It helped me put things into some perspective. I realized my mother wasn't prepared or skilled enough to handle it when I made my announcement. She reacted the only way she knew how.

Our parents gave us all they could. They were not rich, or even well off enough, to give us little extra things smaller families could get. All they had were their children. They took great pride in how they raised us and how we appeared to others. It devastated them when they found out much later, when we were all grown, married, and out of the house, that what they thought they had was tainted by something they had no idea ever happened.

As a child, I could not see how deep my parents' pride was. I am at ease with them now. Even if they had known back then, they wouldn't have had the resources to resolve it and make it all better. It would have ended in destruction for them. The guilt I would have accumulated from that would have been detrimental to me. I already felt I was causing this to happen to me. That extra guilt added on would have blocked any chance of me seeing that I was not their bad little girl who deserved punishing forever.

CHAPTER 3

Fear Not

Next to guilt and shame, fear is one of the dominant emotions that accumulate through an experience like molestation. I lived with many different fears for six or seven years before a whole new lot of fears came about when my brothers finally stopped coming after me.

Unless you are a victim yourself, you may not imagine the deeper fears one goes through while being, and after being, victimized. Nor can many think of the fears that will arise along the road of recovery.

Some fears are obvious and up front. Still, it takes just as much strength to face them and move beyond them. Trust me when I say, with each one faced, you gain so much inner confidence and courage. Even if just a speck of these wonderful qualities is acquired, it is then easier to chip away at the next fear and break through it.

While being molested, victims are afraid of exactly what is being done to them. Anyone can comprehend that one. Fear of the attacker, fear of the physical pain, fear of being beaten if you don't obey, fear of fighting back, even fear of death, in some cases, are common and come to mind easily.

I had them all. Being crushed underneath my much bigger brothers' weight was something I was afraid would happen. It terrified me to think about not being able to break free or that they would never stop. I feared being trapped like an animal in a cage forever. It was somewhat silly perhaps, but real.

I even feared being caught in the act. What was happening was dead wrong. As much as I prayed for someone to stumble upon us,

I feared the embarrassment and humiliation. Most of all I feared no one would believe I didn't want this to happen, or they'd think I had come up with the whole idea. I feared hearing and seeing my mother cry if she knew. Just the same, I feared her reprimanding me if she believed I was the culprit.

Needing to know where my brothers were at all times, I was always looking over my shoulder. They'd pounce like a lion on a steak at each chance one of them had. Through this fear, I developed sensitivity to my surroundings. Not being able to explain it then, I can now. I felt the energy around me change and the air become denser. The back of my neck would tense up, and a chill would go across it. It was as if my brain developed a third ear and a second set of skin just for detecting danger, similar to how a psychic develops a third eye to see more than the average person. With my special radars, I was able to divert my brothers at times or go to another room where the rest of the family was close by to me.

I still get this feeling today. The older I get, the stronger it gets. At times, it happens when people's moods are going to change or an argument is going to break out. If it comes while I'm driving, I change my route or pull over until the feeling subsides. Recently, a very close neighbor of ours passed away. I knew the exact time she died although I wasn't with her.

I felt the change in my body and the air around me. My sensitivity and special power has developed so much that I could hear her talking to me. Unfortunately, it's not so developed that I understood every word. From what I could make out, she was just stopping by to say good-bye. I was so touched that she came to me and we had those last brief few minutes together. It is awkwardly funny how, out of childhood fear, I benefited by developing this unique gift.

Probably, the worst fear I had came during and for many years after the attacks. It stayed until I understood I didn't ask for this to happen and I wasn't guilty or the cause of it in any way. I was petrified beyond belief that I was going to burn in hell. Applying what the nuns and priest preached to us, I knew what was going on was a sin. The fact that it was my entire fault (in my mentality) meant I was an even bigger sinner. It didn't fit in the venial sin category, so it must have been a mortal one. My soul was evil and not worthy of going to heaven with

God. The only place a soul like mine went was hell. I didn't even have a chance of purgatory. I had night terrors about burning alive once I got there. I shook anytime the subject of the devil came up anywhere. I hated Halloween. There was always somebody dressed as the red guy himself. I'd stop in my tracks, for perhaps this time it was the real thing finally coming to get me.

I need to stress again: never was there a time when all three brothers molested me at once. Each took his opportunity separately. Apparently, as I later found out, not one knew about the others. Each and every time one had his way with me, the warning and demand to tell no one was enforced and drilled into me. I don't recall the exact consequences they said would happen if I did tell. Somehow, all the penalties related to being in trouble or being beaten.

Eventually, it became clear to me; it was a bullying and control tactic on their part. They were preying on me just as much mentally as they were physically. Not one but three different people were telling me the same thing. So it must have been truth. I not only feared what would happen if I went against their order, I feared what would happen next after telling on them. Besides, I already had instilled in me that I was going to hell. I didn't need to get in any more trouble.

Nighttime, when I'd have to go to bed, was especially rough for me. I'd fight sleep. When I slept, they were given the chance to sneak in if my sister wasn't there. I didn't sleep for fear I'd stir and find one of them there doing something to me. You know the expression "sleeping with one eye shut"? That was me.

I'd lie there trying not to drift off completely. The Act of Contrition was repeated over and over in my head. I had a lot of sins to be sorry for. Daydreaming was another time-waster. Yep, it is possible, even at night, when it is all dark, to do. I'd imagine fairy godmothers taking me to different families to live with or whisking me off to faraway lands. Prince Charming came once in a while, and we would ride on his white horse, off into the sunset.

When that didn't keep me awake, I'd try predicting all the math problems on the next day's quiz or recite my spelling words and times tables repeatedly. I found counting sheep absolutely useless.

The nights when my bladder would be full were agonizing. I was scared to get up and wander down the hall to the bathroom. Not because of the dark. If one of my brothers heard me getting up, they'd follow me into the bathroom. Like I said, they rarely missed an opportunity. I just knew they were in their beds with one eye and ear open every night also. Rather than give them the chance, when the pain became too unbearable to hold it an anymore, I'd pee the bed and lay in it until morning.

While avoiding sleep, I also feared what the next morning would bring. Guaranteed, with little to no sleep, I was bound to be a miserable brat the next day. At some point, I'd get on somebody's last nerve, and they'd snap. I prayed it would not be an adult because they could give punishments. The nuns would take my recess or lunch time. Worse, if it was Mom, early bedtime was one of her favorite things to serve as punishment. Just what I needed: more time to lie there and avoid sleep. Add up the nights by eight to twelve hours each for at least six years, and your answer is all the sleep I missed out on in life. One can certainly appreciate how I value napping now.

I feared other kids would somehow see through me and figure out why I was different. More horrific, they would announce it to everyone. Afraid of the humiliation and torture, I tried not to speak or go out of my way to be overly friendly. As much as I desired and needed a best friend, I put no effort into looking for one. Best friends shared secrets. I feared having to tell my secret and end up with my best friend hating me.

I found my best friend on October 6, 1984, right before my nineteenth birthday. The minute I saw him, I saw fate fall at my feet. I knew deep in my heart that if I turned and walked (more like ran) to the nearest door, lightning would strike me dead once I got outside. Nothing was worse than lightning. Rather, I battened down the hatches and entered the room where he was sitting. It wasn't long before my hunch about fate and love at first sight were proven correct. We not only became a couple, we became best friends.

I was ecstatic and grateful for finding this friend, but along with it came a responsibility I feared for a long time. I had to tell him of my childhood. We only dated a few weeks before knowing we were going to marry each other. Now, I was really obligated to tell him. He was going to be my husband and deserved to know I came with issues. Morally,

I could not enter a life-long commitment and not have my partner know about the biggest thing in my life and its effects.

I was so scared he wouldn't love me the same, or at all, anymore. The irrational side of my mind was screaming he'd see me as dirty, used, and a whore. The love I yearned so long for was going to leave me because of those three differently gened brothers.

But telling him was more important than my fears. It was the hardest thing I ever had to do in my life. I went through a childhood of shame that felt like it was all lies. I didn't want to have a married life like that also.

Shortly after Christmas that year, we were sitting in his car at a local park, and I took the leap. I just started the conversation. He didn't react all freaky and disgusted by me or what I was saying. He seemed concerned. Tears rolled uncontrollably down my cheeks the entire time, but I just kept talking. He let me get it all out. No one had ever heard me speak of this before, so it seemed as if it took forever. He held my hand and dried my tears. He'd hug me when I needed the encouragement to go on. He cried with me and expressed his sorrow for all the pain I was in. He was honest and said he had no clue how to help me.

But he already had. He let me dump it all out until no more would come out. Even more, he made my fear of him leaving dissolve and didn't run away from me. I vividly remember when I finally got home that night and my head hit the pillow. I went out like a light and slept so serenely, like I never had before. For the first time, I put my full trust in someone when he promised to always love me and never leave. With all the damage I had suffered, it would have been real easy to slip back into my untrusting ways, but when it came to this promise, I have never once doubted it.

The molesting finally stopped in July of 1978. I was twelve and a half years old. I remember the last time any of the three came near me for that purpose. My sister wasn't there anymore. She'd been married for over a year at this point in time. It was a few nights before my oldest brother's wedding. He had been drinking. He had been out at his bachelor party, and the smell of alcohol coming from him was the first clue that awoke me and let me know someone was near my doorway. I held tight to the blankets around me and pretended to be asleep. He came right next to me and whispered drunkenly what he planned to do.

Holding the blankets with clenched white fists so tight the sheet was pushing into my throat, I found out I had bravery in me. I said, *"No!"* Not meek or timid, it was a clear and meaningful reply. My brother must have been equally stunned, or just that intoxicated, for he took a clumsy step back. He said, "What?" rather hesitantly. Again I said, *"No, leave me alone, and don't come near me again."*

He stumbled out of the room. I couldn't do much but sigh with pure and supreme relief. A smile spread across my face, for I felt something so new. I was proud of myself. Never before had I given myself a reason to feel this way.

What a great feeling that I didn't get to revel in for long. Soon returned the fear and waiting for one of them to creep up on me again. Just because I said no once wasn't proof none of them wouldn't try again. This fear remained with me until the last of the three was married and gone from the house.

About a year or so before that last incident, the entire sixth grade class got to learn about the birds and the bees. Boys went in one room to watch a film. The girls went into another room to view theirs. When I went home that day, Mom asked if I had questions and handed me a small book to find answers in if I did have any. Secretly in my room, I paged through the book and absorbed all the information I could. I was astonished, and I swear the earth was shaking as a new fear, worse than going to hell, showered upon me. My brothers' attacks on me had lessened a bit by now. Still it hit me: what they were doing to me all those years could have made me pregnant. Or was I already? Now I didn't eat or sleep for a different fear.

The book stated it takes nine months for a baby to come. So I worried frantically for nine months. When no baby fell out of me, onto the floor, I was able to breathe normally again.

Hey, the book was very vague, and history had proven Mom was not prepared for such subjects. It wasn't in the book, or I missed the important fact, that you need to be menstruating to become pregnant. Count my blessings, I was a late bloomer. But I would have been safe from that unnecessary fear if I had known more facts sooner.

Ironically, out of this fear came my courage to say no that last time. Having some facts of life under my hat, and the fear of having a baby inside me, confirmed the instinct I had all along. They were doing wrong, and it had to stop.

The development of new fears never seemed to stop, though. Married for over a year, I became pregnant. There are list of natural and common fears women experience during pregnancy. Hormones just play with our minds. But I doubt many women fear having a son because he may grow up to be a molester like his uncles. This scared me more than the thought of labor pains. Worse, what if I got pregnant again and it was a girl? I kept dreaming of holding a little baby boy in blue. The fear of bearing a boy subsided. My heart and instinct informed me to let go. I also knew from deep within that the cycle had already ended with me.

Whether it was hormones, mother's instinct kicking in, or something else, I awoke one day knowing as fact it was a little baby girl growing inside me. I stuck very adamantly with the girl hunch the next five months. She was coming out a girl or going back in to finish baking. Of course, I had a girl.

My second pregnancy sadly ended in miscarriage. Blessed a third time, none of the original fears returned, nor did the hunch of boy versus girl. After my first delivery was a complete train wreck and the second ended bitterly, I just kept focus on a safe delivery of a healthy baby, which also happened to be another girl.

Now a mother myself, I faced the fact I most likely would have to tell my daughters of my past. Thinking of this in the mindset of a teen, it didn't seem like it would be an easy discussion. Yet again, here was another fear set upon my plate. How would they react, not only toward me, but toward their uncles and the rest of the family?

In their mid-teens, the time was right. The outcome was okay and not as harsh as I expected. My oldest expressed her sadness and was very glad I had worked through it. My youngest is more sensitive and hotheaded, unlike the first. I had to approach the subject with her in a different manner. It was up to me to have her understand first there was no need for revenge or retaliation. Before I could even speak of the past, I had to make extremely clear I was over and way beyond the hurt and agony and I didn't want her to dig up the past. Those ideas of revenge had passed long ago, and I never wanted them. My little one needed to be reassured that her mommy was not hurting anymore. Once she was positive of this, she asked many more questions than her sister had. In adult terms, they had a better understanding of me as their mother and who and why I am. In a teenager's term, to sum it up, they were cool with it.

In regards to my brothers, I still feared them after the abuse ceased, but in a different way. It wasn't what they would or could do to me. It was the emotions they were capable of stirring in me when I'd see them at family functions. All the emotions were negative. Hatred, anger, insecurity, inferiority are just a few examples. It seemed every time I made progress to feel better about myself, I'd encounter them. They seemed happy and content. Life just went on its merry old way for them. Not for me, though. I had this phobia that I was doomed and destined to be miserable and haunted by them all my life.

I had numerous questions that I'd ask myself each time I had one of these setbacks or flashbacks, questions only they held the answers to. Basic ones like: Do they regret it? Do they remember? Did they hate me? The last one is a bit funny. They should have been posing that question to me.

I frequently had the flashback of one particular attack. The words my brother whispered in my ear were inerasable, forever etched on my brain. He said that he wished I wasn't his sister. Every time my memory recalled his statement, I questioned if that was what he still wished for.

I feared the answers no matter what they may have been. The questions rolled around in my brain any day, every day, anytime, and all the time. I couldn't stop them. The racing thoughts drove me delirious occasionally.

More than the answers, I feared hearing the questions come from my lips. This would mean I was in front of them, possibly alone, verbalizing what I pondered deeply. Never would I be that brave to confront any one of them. But given time, I could just prove myself wrong on that thought.

CHAPTER 4

Give Me a Break, Teen Years Are Hard Enough

As I mentioned in the first chapter, my teen years were ghastly. The added pressure of being molested intensified the fated awkward years.

The molestation had stopped, but I felt no better. I was burdened by tremendous guilt and fear related to everyone and everything around me. I pictured myself as dirty, worthless, ugly, and repulsive. Consequent to that, I drew within myself and put an ultrathick shell around me. Isolated and lost, I went about each day in a cocoon made of steel. Still there was no one I could talk with. Actually, there was not one person I trusted to reveal my secret to.

One of the farms about a mile up the highway was sold. New townhomes were constructed shortly after the sale, when I was a freshman in high school. My younger brother was the adventurer. He was the baby of the family, which meant rules set in stone evaporated away when he came of age to practice them. Before I knew it, he was on his bike, up and across the highway, finding friends in the new section of homes.

He also convinced our mother I needed to go with him one day. Never wanting to hang with me, he was up to something. Of course, one of his new buddies had a sister. She was my brother's age, two years younger than I was. It was my job to hang with the sister to free the boys up so they could go ride bikes in the woods or whatever it was that boys did when sisters weren't tagging along.

Luckily for my little brother, she and I become closer friends. As more houses were built, the neighborhood grew, and so did our circle of friends. This was definitely a first for me. Girls and guys alike, we hung out together.

I wasn't particularly close to anyone in the sense of connected souls. There were many differences between them and me. Age, for one. I was the oldest girl. I believe I was the only if not one of the rare few living with both my original parents. The biggest difference was they were all street smart and I was rather naive. Blending fully with them never seemed to happen. I knew from the bottom of my gut this wasn't where I'd be for the rest of my life. Nevertheless, I continued walking up the highway every day to be with them.

They were my escape, escape from home, escape from a house where every room flashed bad memories again and again. I needed them, so I stayed where my heart recognized there were no answers for me. Beyond this little posse of mine, there was no social involvement for me. There were no activities to join in. Public transportation to get to where they did have them didn't exist in our area. And I was a misfit amongst the nose-in-the-air snobs at school who had rich parents. Being that I didn't have blonde hair and attention-getting breasts, cheerleading wasn't an alternative either.

Soon this street-smart group was bored sitting around chilling. They became street active and started to involve themselves with street life. My inner voice was telling me to run from it. Instead of listening, I convinced myself to try to fit in a bit more.

I tried some idiotic things to be more like them and not stand out like the sore thumb. First attempt was to start smoking. Yeah, I was cool, and for appearances' sake, I was one of them. All that I really achieved was a nasty, sickening habit.

Next attempt was a complete disaster. Cigarettes became old news. Pot was the new "cool." I resisted for a long time. Eventually I had to give in and take a few hits to keep fitting in and not lose my escape, my friends. Everyone else became mellow and went off to a realm of no worries. Not me. I was a mess. Paranoia and the jitters came over me. My heart raced super fast and seemed to have no rhythm.

The two girls I would pal around with had seen it happen. We concluded it was my first time, and my nerves had caused the bad effect. Naturally, there was a second time I smoked marijuana with them. I ended up with the same effects to a higher degree. This time, as I walked up the highway toward home, alone, that evening, I was swinging at cars passing by. The headlights were spies coming to kidnap me. Thank the heavens I made it home okay. I put myself in what could have been a much worse situation for the sake of keeping appearances and my reputation. Never again did I go near the stuff. My friends accepted my decision.

Drinking went hand in hand with the weed. When allowances were good, my friends would chip in for a six-pack or two. Even though cigarettes and pot were failed attempts, I was dumb enough to try drinking. Anything was better than being stuck at home. I started chipping in to get my own share of the packs. I wonder if any of them ever noticed that a beer would last me the entire night.

My girlfriends met some older guys who lived across the highway in their own apartment. Rather than have to face being home, I took them up on the extended invitation to go across to the complex and party with these fellas. Once again, I should have followed my gut and not put my better judgment to the curb.

These guys had their own keg in the middle of the kitchen floor. I figured I could nurse a glass like I did the bottles every other weekend. The glass lasted me a few hours. As soon as it was empty, another appeared in front of me. I was already feeling tired and a wee buzzed from the first. I took a few sips of the new one and don't remember much after that. Not until I was pushed out the passenger side of a car onto my front lawn. The fuzzy spin in my head stopped for a brief few seconds, so I could see my mom and one of my brothers at the front door.

How I made it to my bed, no clue. I awoke to the walls and bed spinning around me. I spent the next twelve hours vomiting nonstop. As much as I tried to recall the night before, I couldn't catch a glimpse. To this day, there is a beginning and an end, but no middle. It freaked me out not knowing. My friends assured me nothing bad had happened, but I was filled with unease by the missing time gap. Most of all, I was angry with myself for not listening to that voice in my head that told me not to go.

My drinking and partying days were over. I sucked at it. The loss of control over my body and mind made me sure of this. I still hung with the group, but steered clear of alcohol. I was approaching high school graduation, and my view of being part of the gang was slowly changing.

Probably due to the two-or three-year age difference, sitting around watching everyone else drink and get high wasn't thrilling enough to me anymore. Gradually, other drugs came around. I wasn't going down that road. That lifestyle was headed nowhere good, and that wasn't what I had in mind for myself. In my heart I knew I was capable of better, even though my self-image told me different. Actually, I had nothing in mind of where I was headed in life, but I knew hanging out wasn't helping me make any progress.

A few years ago, I ran into one of the girls from our circle, and she caught me up in where everyone was at that point in time. She herself had had her share of trials, tribulations, and successes over the years. Overall, she seemed happy, and I was glad for her. For the majority, it seemed most of them realized at about the same age I did that it was time for more than hanging with friends.

Sadly, things did not fall into place or work out so well for a few. Hearing the news that one of the guys I dated for a good period of time killed himself devastated me. He had the willpower, mind-set, and ego to be anything he wanted to be. I will never know why he chose to end his life. Surely, there was something eating at him underneath it all that he could not heal or overcome. Back then, I connected with his mother immensely. She was a leftover flower child from years gone by, still being one of the kids in more than one way. She did share with me some things that happened in her childhood and past that were very tragic. She suffered from depression, and I recall her going away to the hospital a few times. Although she never openly admitted to the depression, somehow I knew. I sensed parts of me in her. Shortly after her son's death, she committed suicide also. I pray often that whatever it was that tormented both of them is gone and they are both at peace now.

One of the other boys in particular stood out as different from the rest. I admired his charm and upbeat approach to everyday life. He saw things with deeper meaning than the rest. He'd find something positive even about the most boring night sitting around with some of the gang on the curb in the complex. In his eyes, something was always awesome with the most mundane of things. It was a nice surprise to run into him about eight years ago. He told me where he was living, and I recognized the address as a half-way recovery house here in my town. He was the last person I'd ever expect to become an alcoholic. Shocked at first, I realized we all had our problems in life. Perhaps we were all brought together as one big group to give each other the opportunity to move on and tackle the things haunting us. Today, I still consider him a friend. He is eight and a half years sober. I am as proud of him as I am of myself.

Not to sound conceited or snobbish, but putting the distance between me and my friends proved better for me. They were my diversion to home, but I am grateful I followed my instincts and broke away and did not remain in my rut. Equally, I am just as grateful all our paths crossed. None of them knew I was molested or what was going on inside my head, but they helped me learn about myself. It was because of them that I reached the next step in recovery. It took me years to comprehend what they brought to my life.

Following my intuition prevented me from gaining serious addictions. Having made drugs or alcohol my outlet, I would have only clouded and expanded my issue of being molested. I desperately needed to face the matters hovering over me alone and unattached to anything or anyone else. Going off in one of my daydreams, I realized how strange it was that my attempts with marijuana and alcohol went bad. It was as if someone, like a guardian angel, was behind the scenes causing mayhem to protect me.

As I graduated, I did a major amount of thinking. Spending less time with the group freed up time for me to think of where I was to go next. I'd spend hours in deep thought playing the "what-if's" and "how could's." I would travel far into my own little world. No answers came, and the helpless and secluded feeling was stronger than ever. My mind was an endless Ferris wheel ride that spun faster than the real thing. I had already spent a good majority of my teen years avoiding my molestation and dwelling on it at the same time. It didn't seem like anything would change soon.

Feelings about myself hadn't changed at all. I was still worthless, low, undeserving, stupid, and so on. Note that none of my feelings were ever positive. Kicking my own butt was a daily thing. I'd beat myself up for wasting all that time with friends and not thinking of the future. Actually, I'd bully myself for not even seeing a glimpse of the future. If I spilled a cup of tea on the table, I would belittle myself because I could not do anything right. Something as minute as accidentally putting my shirt on backward would trigger a whole epilogue of words in which I did nothing but berate myself. Negative self-talk was a skill I perfected rather brilliantly. Most of all I beat myself up the most over whatever it was I did to deserve being molested. Years after, I still placed the blame on me.

I was at my lowest point. I considered killing myself very briefly, but had no confidence in myself to do it. I'd screw it up somehow. Then there was the wish to crawl under a rock and stay there for eternity. Just my luck, I couldn't find a rock big enough.

I placed more blame on myself than my brothers for how miserable my life was. I blamed my friends for not seeing through me, helping, and accepting me more. Furthermore, I aimed fault on my mother. After all, she hadn't listened to me all those years ago. Nor did she utter one word when I came home that night so drunk and wasted.

I began comparing my friends to my brothers. Mostly, I resented them all. It was impossible to differentiate who was making me feel what. I could see myself becoming nastier with myself, never toward them. It wasn't in my nature to hurt people intentionally. Doing so would make me open game for return treatment. I certainly wasn't one to stir the pot for fear my past history would come out.

In one of my trips to my little world of deep thought, it hit me. Everything that happened to me was making the unhappy person I was. Deeper yet, I realized it was going to make me the person I'd be as an adult.

It was hugely obvious that it wasn't making me a good person. At last, I saw a glimpse into my future. I was to be a mean, critical, hateful wench who used and abused those around her, living and dying a slow death with not a soul to miss her. *Dear Lord, don't let me be that,* I thought.

Seeing this hag with all her rotten qualities, I knew immediately I had to find the good in me or get some somehow. At this point, all I saw when I looked at my reflection in the mirror was a seventeen-year-old girl who had somehow asked to be molested. That single-handedly caused all the negative things I believed myself to be. It also helped these negative things to grow and become reality. I tried to find the good in me every single day, but as I was consumed to the point of being obsessive-compulsive, no answers came immediately.

A diploma under my belt and eighteen, I hadn't the vaguest idea of what type of career to reach for. Although, it was almost the mid-eighties, the nuns at my all-girl high school still hadn't caught on to Women's Lib. There was no encouragement to "be what you want to be." Unless you were one of the geniuses in the class, no one let on that college existed. All the rest of us were to take steno and typing classes to become better secretaries and typists. Yuck. Sitting at a desk all day was not a vision I saw myself doing. I was left in limbo with a diploma and no direction to head.

Eventually, I took a job as a pharmacy technician. Back then, it was on-the-job training. No schooling was required. I was nervous and very uncomfortable around people. Fumbling over words was a frequent experience. Working the front counter, I greeted many sick people and handled the phones. This was similar to the bartender who hears all the sad sagas from his patrons. The difference being, I felt like a blubbering fool. The word "idiot" jumped out in my brain every time a customer left after telling me their woes. All I could say at the time was, "Aw, that's so sad," several times during the conversation. My skills of adding to a conversation lacked as much as my confidence. Deep down, I believed customers had shared the same opinion of me that I did.

Two months after starting, my boss stood next to me as I counted out pills on a teal green plastic tray. Out of the blue, he began talking to me. I was flabbergasted by what I was hearing him say. I kept looking over my shoulder to see if he was really talking to another employee, but we were the only two in the back pharmacy area. He was commending me on how I treated customers. More surprising were the words he described me with. He used words like, "honest," "fair," "friendly," "compassionate," and "a will to learn." Not used to hearing compliments or any positive descriptive referring to me, I thought he was off his rocker. However, having manners, I thanked him anyway, especially when he put forth a nice raise.

Home alone in my room that evening, I kept running those words through my mind. Daydreaming mode set in. This time I didn't have to make up a scene to go with the words. I replayed the time an elderly woman came in and was crying because she had just lost her husband. I went around the counter with tissues and sat holding her hand until she was done.

I told her I did not know what to say, other than I was sorry she was so sad. Aha, I was compassionate and honest. I continued daydreaming and finding times when I did show these qualities. I had no choice but to agree with my boss. I did have good qualities in me.

Down deep, I was aware I was all the things he said. The negative feelings I had were so much at the forefront that all the positive ones got pushed down to the bottom for a long while. Compare this to homemade soup. (My mom did make fabulous chicken noodle soup.) Without doubt, the fat and yucky stuff always comes to the top. You cannot stop what is bound to happen. Naturally and eventually, someone comes along and skims that scummy stuff from the surface. This leaves you with all the good, yummy stuff in the bottom. At first spoonful, you hesitantly like what you taste. Another spoonful, and you are anxious for some more. You begin to love and praise it and the cook, until every drop is gone. You are left with all these ingredients of goodness in your stomach. You leave the table comforted just by knowing all this goodness is in your belly. You sometimes feel so good that you stay for seconds. All in all, you can always remember how good you felt and look forward to the next time.

I now had some better qualities to work with. My opinion of myself was a tad improved. It was really hitting home that it was possible to be a good person. My social life picked up a bit too.

The girls from work would get together at night. We would go to a restaurant/bar and sit for hours snacking, conversing, and listening to the local bands. We weren't of age to drink, and even if I could have, I had no desire. Dance clubs were our stomping grounds also. I loved to dance but remained a wallflower while my friends made good use of the dance floor. Self-confidence was still lacking. Dancing was for the privacy of my bedroom. To get up in public wasn't possible yet.

While out and about, few guys approached me and offered a dance, let alone a date. When dates were offered, I'd usually accept, being they were so rare. I'd accept because of my inadequacies also. I didn't think anyone would want to date me to begin with. I believed I would never find better and still believed I didn't deserve better.

I dated some real creeps. They were younger, equal to, and one was even twenty-nine years older than me. Few had second or third dates by my choice. The only nice one of the bunch was a mama's boy. He was around for six months before going off to the military.

Whether it was one night out together or two, the guys all had something in common. They had no problem putting me, or females in general, down. They were conceited, obnoxious, and rather cocky. Their attitudes alone dampened their chance of a second date or a friendship.

Furthermore, with each and every one, I got the instinct they only wanted one thing—sex. The thought revolted me. I wasn't a piece of meat, and I had had enough of that growing up. Flashbacks of my brothers molesting me appeared. Rather than let these dates go to the point of sex, I would find some excuse to go home and flee.

No matter how I looked at it, they didn't make me feel good or have any beneficial effect toward improving my self-image. This time I listened to my inner voice and didn't attempt further contact with these jerks.

Without knowing, I was starting to set serious standards for myself. I made my own personal pact: no more dating unless they fit my ideals of a date or partner. I pictured in my mind the date one of my old classmates brought to our freshman date dance. We met for no more than ten minutes. However, in that brief amount of time, he made a lasting impression. He treated his date like a lady. He genuinely cared and was interested in our conversation. He also took interest in her friends. He offered to get her a soda. It was evident that he respected her. He even took the time to buy her the prettiest yellow tea roses that accessorized and matched her dress perfectly.

This was what I wanted, and I was determined to reject anything less. I prayed that I would meet someone like this. By now my ideas of not deserving better were fading. Those good things I had in me should have earned me more than bottom-of-the-barrel dates. I held high hopes my prayer would be answered.

Heaven didn't drop any fitting prospects in my lap, so dating ceased for a while. Out of boredom, I would head up the highway and visit the old gang. Not much had changed. They did extend an invitation to a surprise birthday party one of the girls' boyfriends was throwing for her. It went in one ear and out the other. A week later, my two friends showed up at my house to take me with them. I had completely forgotten about it and was shocked to see them. In truth, I did not feel well, but there was no hearing of not going.

They stripped me of my pajamas, raided my closet, dressed me, did my makeup and hair, and scooted me right out to the car. We arrived at the party house. We were directed to go down the hall, into a family room with the other guests. Giving me no chance to stall, my friends pushed me down the hall.

That is when I turned the corner into the room and there he was. I tried to turn back to run, and my friends grabbed me. They were telling me to go in. I was saying, "No way, he's in there, and if I go in, I'll leave with him and marry him." Of course they thought I was absolutely nuts and shoved me into the room.

The guy whose image I compared to all other potential dates was right there in the flesh. I avoided him until he asked the birthday girl to introduce us. He was perfect. My friends found it so amusing they ditched me. This enabled him to come to my rescue and give me a lift home later that night. He was a gentleman. I didn't even have to fight off an attempt on his part for a goodnight kiss.

God had given me a response to my prayers. Better than meeting my fantasy date, I re-met the guy who had escorted my classmate to the date dance all those years ago. Once again, my instinct was correct. We did get married. Twenty-some years later, I'm still laughing at the irony. Fate surely has a sense of humor and likes to catch us off guard. Words cannot express how thankful I am for my friends who gave me the fifteen-minute miracle makeover and the push, literally and spiritually, that I was in dire need of.

As humans, we often send out our prayers only to be discouraged when we do not hear a reply. One of the most important lessons I have learned in life is about those responses we seek. God and the heavens rarely speak back. It is up to us to be open for the answers. Response to our prayers comes visually, mentally, through a feeling in our souls and/or physical bodies. We have to just trust and have faith that an answer will come. Pondering or insisting upon a reply does nothing but hinder our ability to see the answer we are expecting.

Now that I had not just a date, but a true boyfriend, much of the negativity I felt about myself was put on the back burner. Sure, the negativity was still there, but he had a way of making me forget about it most of the time. Life had truly taken a turn up the right road for once. I was looking forward to marriage and sharing the rest of my life trying to equal the love he showed and gave to me. I even decided on a career somewhat. I decided I wanted to become a mother.

CHAPTER 5

Insight

Throughout the previous pages, I've mentioned how my insight or instincts moved me forward in a positive direction. I was very fortunate at a very young age to have these qualities. However, both had to be developed. Equally I had to learn to listen to what I was discovering. Too often I fought it or chose to ignore what was smack in front of my face.

I've never been sure if I gained my insight and talent for getting hunches from being molested or it came with me at birth. Either way, it's been a gift that has proven beneficial rather regularly. I lean more to being born with it. I want to believe we are all born with these skills to some degree. Obstacles like daily life and other aspects, such as our surroundings, our emotional level and our ability to process thoughts get in the way for some of us to develop it to the point of being a daily tool.

All in all, I am grateful to have them. They have saved me many a time from making bad choices. It not only became useful in overcoming the issues of being molested, but it's helped me in financial choices, judging peoples' characters, and avoiding situations that could have turned out to be a nasty situation. This intuitive nature has helped me decipher when someone was not being truthful and possibly had ulterior motives.

For the most part, these special traits have helped me find out just who I am. As far as dealing with my brothers, I did not have to seek professional help for the most part. When I needed answers, they were really in me before I posed my questions. It was my insight and gut reactions that brought the answers forth for me to see. I am not saying don't reach out to a therapist or psychologist to find answers. Run to them, by any means you have, if you need release from issues that burden and inhibit you. The average person cannot do it alone. In my case, I was capable of doing for myself what a professional would do. The funny side of this is I had no idea how I was helping myself or the impact it made on my outlook.

Having the insight to see that being molested would destroy me or make me at such an early age is extremely rare. At least that is what some professionals have told me. One or more has lost composure and looked astonished when they hear how I recovered. They cannot comprehend that I did it mostly through thinking it through. They have had patients well into adult years who can't grasp what I figured out so early. My heart aches for those patients who never move forward.

The more I hated myself and just wanted to disappear, the louder that voice in my head informed me to keep going. When I got a strong instinct like this, I would cling to it. It was habit to repeat it over and over to myself. It didn't stop until I thought about every aspect of an idea that would pop into my head out of nowhere. I would toss it around and apply it to my life until every puzzle piece fit. Not before then would I fully believe in it. It took many accomplishments of realizing the tiniest aspect to chip away slowly at the burden I carried.

Take for instance the quote by John Harrigan on a little plaque that came in a set I purchased from one of those home demonstrations. Only in my young twenties at the time, I will ponder this one forever. Today I try to recall it when I have a rough time dealing with someone who is on my wrong side: "People need loving the most when they deserve it the least." That one mouthful of words packs a real punch.

When first reading it, I thought of how sweet it was. Once it was on my wall, where I could see it from every angle of the room, it kept pulling me. I must have read it a thousand times. One day I sat and really read it. I did my daydreaming thing and applied this quote to myself. I realized that I did deserve to be loved. The doubt that I was worthy of love still lingered in the back of my mind. One little saying, thought through, brought me to the realization I had earned what love I had around me. Most of the love I had at this point came from my wonderful husband. Any doubt that I belonged with him fled like a burglar in the night.

The quote popping out at me didn't stop there. I started directing it toward other people in my life. The conclusion came: everyone, no matter your present, past, or future is deserving of love. It was a little harder to agree when I applied it to my molesters. Looking at them back then, I didn't feel they deserved anything at all. When I connected the quote with their present lives, it was tough to not let the past interfere. Thinking of only their current lives, I had to admit, they deserved to be loved also. They were good dads, husbands, and worked hard. I had no choice but to give credit where it was due. But hell would have to freeze over before I'd consider them deserving forgiveness.

A little hard to swallow, I struggled with the fact that they needed to be loved as much as I. I combated the realization as much as possible. I hated them having something so positive, but one more time my gut won out. I had to remember that had I also fought hard not to be a mean and vengeful person. My heart told me if I didn't accept, I'd be undoing what I had worked so hard to become. I had to give in to reason and admit my brothers may have done some horrible things, but they were still deserving of love.

A lot of recovery tactics came to me when I was twenty. It was then that I came to the conclusion that I wasn't at fault for what my brothers had chosen to force upon me. I assured myself that I did not ask for them to molest me. No action of mine gave them reason to either. I was free of guilt. I can't think of what caused this to just explode into my head one day. It wasn't a TV show, quote, or daydreaming that brought it on. Truly, it had to be some mysterious unknown force that enlightened me this time.

My guilt was gone, but I still had bushels of blame to put in place. Where to direct that blame took some more thinking. I always felt guilty for finding my parents at fault. Through all the years when I put that spotlight on them, I always felt ashamed for directing any negativity toward them. That nagging little voice kept telling me they weren't responsible, but I shut it up because I was angry. Given the chance, I would have blamed the milkman if it made me feel less bitter. Truthfully, the more I found others guilty, the angrier and more stressed I became. Yes, my parents were naive and blind to my suffering, but they were not the cause of my torture and torment. In my heart and soul, I believe, if they had more knowledge of what was happening, they would have reacted on my behalf.

Once I removed my parents from the list of possible suspects, I was left with my three brothers. Free to point fingers, I aimed directly at them. With all other garbage and obstacles aside, in the end, they were responsible for their actions. No one was making them do this. All of them were of age to know right from wrong. Plus, they all had a Catholic education like I did. They could not deny being taught about sins and The Commandments. If it wasn't a sin or simply wrong, there wouldn't have been a need for them to tell me to keep it a secret.

I began to think maybe they didn't have consciences. Maybe it wasn't genes, after all, that made them different. I began to feel sorry for them. I stopped that train wreck of thought rather quickly. I wasn't giving them the benefit of the doubt. They had a conscience as well as I did. They all knew what they were doing. No way was I going to give in and give them pity, especially after all this time. The whole kit and kaboodle, all the blame was theirs.

It is somewhat indescribable the uplifting energy you gain when you remove guilt from your shoulders. This energy was equally physical and mental. My mind was so much clearer to think freely and focus. The guilt had managed to fog my brain with an abundance of added issues and feelings. The guilt was what was weighing me down from making progress in overcoming my torments.

My mental sense changed for the better. My self-opinion was improved. My belief had been that I was an ugly ogre who should have been caged or banished. Now when I looked in the mirror, I could bear to look at my reflection, for it really wasn't all that bad. I began to see fully that I was a loving, likeable, and honorable person. The feeling of complete strangers staring at me in public and my past being obvious to them subsided. I could go to the mall, purchase something as simple as socks, and feel comfortable in my own shell. The negative self-talk I spoke all too often diminished a great deal. When it did come up, I could usually combat it with a positive response about myself.

Physically, I became much more active. I found craft projects a favorite escape from work.

When my husband was off, I looked forward to going out and socializing or having friends visit. The nervousness of how I appeared or sounded to others didn't get in the way of me getting to know them. I really felt like I belonged and was accepted by others also. No longer was I the wallflower who arrived late and fled to a corner to be unnoticed. Friends and family had probably taken me to be either shy or snobbish due to my lack of verbalization. Little did they know not being very talkative was a side effect of fear, lack of self-confidence, and shame.

Suddenly, the phone was attached to my ear like a teenage girl. I had missed out on that essential part of my adolescence. It amazed me that people wanted to talk to me too. The fact that they approached me gave me the added boost and influenced my self-worth. My spirits were lifted with each ordinary chat. I stilled lacked in the confidence department for many more years, but things were on a forward path finally.

The change was felt within me. No one ever mentioned that they saw a difference, but surely they could. My physical appearance was the same. It was deep inside me that was different. There was this ever so petite glowing light coming from my center and radiating out of me. I could feel myself shining. My path of life seemed to be sprinkled with rose petals.

Motherhood soon came along. My recovery slowed to dribs and drabs due to diapers. Anyone who has ever taken on the duties of a caregiver of another understands this.

I struggled between two motherly duties: one, to protect my child from similar harm, and two, to provide the nourishment as I had as much as the nurturing that was void in my early years.

Considering my childhood history, very easily I could have become the overprotective and overly obsessive mother. The fear of my own children having the same or similar experiences almost gave me the right to hover and darn near smother them. For their sakes, I realized even during pregnancy that I would have to find a balance of protection. Without the rational or even-keeled amount, I'd end up with rebellion from my offspring. Down the road, the result would be me feeling like a failure.

In order to nurture them as I wanted, I had to allow them some leeway and open space. This meant I had to let down my guard and protectiveness a speck. It would have been so simple to command and always step forth to keep them safe, but my children would become stifled mentally. All they would know was my opinions and emotions. I couldn't do that to them. Instead, I would allow them to develop their own feelings and the right to their own opinions.

We all experience, or as parents, we see our kids experience, a bully in the neighborhood or schoolyard. My oldest daughter's chance came when she was six years old. Her personality was quiet, meek, and kind. She had been out playing and came running in, frantic and upset that another girl was pushing her around. Impulse wanted me to step in to give the bully a good lecture and march her back up the street to her mother. Mature rationalization told me to hold off. Sense took over, and I did wait. I listened to my daughter and dried her tears. I encouraged her to go back out and face her fear: the bully.

Day after day, my daughter went back out and attempted to resolve things with the other child. Things improved for a little while, until the bully went back to her old ways. This time I did go to the mother. I even wondered, by me approaching her, if she would, in turn, bully me. In a way, I had to overcome a small fear also. It all worked out in the end. The bully received a lecture and punishment from both her parents. My daughter and the other girl soon began building their friendship.

You know how they say the third time is a charm. The next time this girl acted up was her last chance from my daughter. This time my daughter responded to the tormenting by simply walking away. She came home and was able to express to me that this girl didn't make her feel good about herself. She also commented that this girl wasn't being a friend and didn't deserve to have her as one. If out of my own fears I had taken over and made things all better in the beginning, my daughter would have missed out on a valuable lesson. Today my oldest, as well as my youngest, see respect as that two-way street. They expect it as much as they give it in regards to friendship and other relationships.

Just recently, I received a wonderful compliment from my daughter's boss. She expressed to me that it is a joy to be around her. Unlike many teens she encounters, she is very responsible and respectful. Most of all, she thanked me for raising such a well-rounded child, for sharing her and allowing her to work for the company.

I smiled from ear to ear. It is moments like these that I am so grateful for the insight I had to not push my fears onto my children and to let them spread their wings.

To imagine where I'd be without my strong sense of intuition sends shivers up my spine.

I would have never made one step of progress without it. I would have never grown to know myself, let alone my husband and daughters. I would not be here telling you that there are better days to come, or that even the most haggard of days or weeks can have a positive effect at a later date.

I came across a quote by actor Alan Alda. He said, "You have to leave the city of your comfort and go into the wilderness of your intuition. What you'll discover will be wonderful. What you'll discover is yourself." I connected to what he was saying.

There were many times I had to go outside my comfort zone and see where intuition led me. In some sense, I was testing my own intuition to prove it right or wrong. Oddly, it was the same gut-wrenching instinct that would tell me to follow the original insight and give it a chance.

It was easy being bitterly miserable and resenting my brothers. That was my way. For the most part, I was stuck on being that way until I saw how important it was to change. It was nature taking its course on my mental sense and physical reactions to the situation being molested had dealt me. Given more time, the negativity ejected out of me would have been much deeper and stronger.

Previously in this chapter, I wrote about my revelation of people deserving love. To benefit from the insights regarding this, I had to remove myself from what was familiar to me, put all negativity aside, and think it out rationally. In the end, I discovered that if I needed to change my outlook. Not doing so, would make me hypocritical and biased.

Thinking back over some of the little steps of progress I've taken over the years, the realization of what Mr. Alda's quote means for me becomes clear. No matter how an instinct got into my brain, I had to explore it. Look at it from different angles. See it from different sides. Put aside my previous opinions. Even think of what others' perspective would be on it. Simply ignoring it just meant it would keep coming back. I would get no peace from an insight until I looked it square in the face. Taking it on as soon as it came to me saved me half the battle. But when complete, the insight was always proven right, and I was glad that I had followed.

Furthermore, it is so true that, by exploring your intuitions, you find yourself. I have discovered so much about me. I am not an ugly ogre unworthy of love. I am not guilty. I am a person worthy of love, as well as one ready and willing to extend love to others. I am capable of being a friend, spouse, and parent. I am someone who others can rely on and place their trust in. These are just some of the things I would never believe myself to be if I had never learned to trust my intuition. I now listen to what my gut says, unless somewhere along the line I get another hunch that tells me the first one was off track.

My insights have left me with many positive effects and feelings about numerous situations and people. Once I accepted that my mind wasn't playing head games, my intuition became an essential tool of my recovery. The key to it being a successful tool was to use it and let it lead me to where I was destined to go, for my insights were only answers that I already knew that were buried deep within my soul.

In Chapter One, I noted that I practice astrology with my friends. Once again, I realize not everyone agrees with it. I'm open to others' opinions, but by checking out to see what all the skepticism is about, I found a different point of view on the subject. I'm not a guru or fanatic. I don't let it rule my life either. Instead, I use it as a guide to understand and better myself.

It amazes me every time I look at my natal or birth chart. That's the map of where all the planets and zodiac signs were the moment I was born. What it states about my personality and relationships with others is extremely precise. It just as accurately denotes major events in my life. It even says I would have a strong sense of intuition and I would use it for good. Well if I wasn't a believer after seeing all this spread out before my eyes, then this next thing would surely have had me hooked. In the area that depicts siblings, it told that my relationship with my brothers would be affected by trauma, hardships, and avoidance starting in early childhood. Furthermore, this relationship would be the cause of wounds I would need to find out how to heal. I would learn many life lessons in the area of siblings.

In the areas that denote childhood and my parents (especially the mother), my chart proved true again. I would be cared for, but there would be a distance in our relationship. All of it fit the picture of my life so far.

Looking at my natal chart and the information it provides me makes me wonder. Did I plan this all out ahead of time with God? Is this the plan he had for me? Did I choose this ahead of time before being born? How did all the stars all end up in the place they were so that this is what my chart tells me? Once again, I fall upon my insight for answers. It doesn't matter if it was pre-planned or coincidence. I believe in my instinct that this was all meant to be. I was to experience what I have in order to grow into who I was to become. It was up to me to find the ways within myself to strive for good and not evil. Somehow, my experiences in childhood were to become my purpose, my theme, my true test in this lifetime.

CHAPTER 6

Taking Control

Before becoming a mother, my outlook on my molestation was definitely negative. There were bad memories, bad feelings, and bad side effects. The negatives buried my self-confidence, self-worth, spirit, and drive to live life. It took a lot to get to the point where I realized I was deserving of good things. It wasn't until then that I began to experience life.

Even with that leap of progress, all the bad memories and haunting questions lingered. They floated in my mind like little bubbles that were dark and eerie. Each bubble represented a different torment. When one would pop, it would burst and fill the air around me and my day with gloom. My mood would depreciate, and I was brought down. I'd fight with myself to push the bubbles away to regain balance again. This may have taken me from a few moments to a few days.

I assumed this was a natural process of recovery. Two steps forward, one and a half back, leaving me with just a half step ahead. It wasn't much, but I would take credit where credit was due. It was still progress and not remission or a failure. Although I bounced back and forth, I always held hope that my time on the downside would be short. I held higher hope that someday I'd bounce back to the good side of things and never bounce backward again.

Entering the adventurous world of parenthood didn't change what happened to me, nor did it cure me. In a peculiar way, parenthood eased some aspects and intensified others. One great effect was I now had this little creation who loved me for me. I loved her back with awe.

My past never came into question. Each time I looked into my little girl's eyes, I was reminded that this was a brand new relationship and beginning. She not only brought me love, she caused pure happiness, satisfaction, and pride in my world. These were feelings that I had never much experienced in life, with the exception of meeting, dating, and marrying my husband.

It wasn't until three years later that I was blessed with my second daughter. It amazed me that it was just as joyous as the first time. In a way, because this was the second time around, I expected it to be familiar and old hat. Yes, it was, but all the same exhilaration was there too. My days and nights were filled with first teeth, first steps, and first words. It was full-time work plus overtime. Every second was worth it.

The birth of my two children and my wedding were the three greatest things to happen in my life. Unfortunately, as powerful and positive as these events were, they could not wipe out my childhood memories and trauma.

All the flashbacks and thoughts were still there. Those tiny bubbles did not float away while I was in labor and delivery. I'd be in the middle of folding a load of Onesies and booties and along came a bubble that would just appear and burst. My mood would be dampened. I became agitated and irritated. At times, I'd become nauseous or shaky. It was a challenge to try to regain my senses and be a mom at the same time. The memories consumed me. My will was to keep focus on my children, but my past kept interfering.

Not a day went by that I didn't deal with both. There was no balance, in a sense. I just coped.

Common everyday tasks were hard to complete. Being drawn by the negative thoughts, I at times just went through the motions of daily chores and care of my girls. It was the best I was capable of at the time. I was multitasking and responsible for two major concerns, my children and my recovery, that competed for my attention. Looking back, I don't know how I managed to function. To be honest, I felt more dysfunctional than anything else.

In no way was I a bad mother, nor did I neglect my daughters. Both my girls always had my full attention. It was just that, mentally, my mind would be elsewhere. We did everything together. I was that mom who let them dig in with their own hands when I baked. Fingerpaints,

Play-Doh, and mud pies were habits, not treats. Any way I could encourage their imagination, I tried it. Blanket forts took over our living room. To someone looking in, they would get the impression that my house was the *Romper Room*.

Mealtime was no exception. They always ate healthily and had fun doing it. I think that's why, as they grew, they weren't afraid to try new things and had few dislikes. I drew flowers and shapes with ketchup. Pancakes weren't round. They were poured into letter shapes, so they could learn their ABC's. I was always thinking up a new way to spark their imagination, interest, and intellect.

I loved being a mother. I felt I finally had a purpose in life, rather than the feeling of being an unraveled ball of yarn that kept getting in others' way and tripping them up. My daughters depended on me and looked to me for guidance and praise. It was a strange contradiction. Here I was, shaping the lives of two small children, yet my own life seemed to be in disarray due to my molestation.

I was just plain old tired of battling with my childhood. I was frustrated that it kept coming back to torment me. Screaming inside, I'd yell, *Go away! Can't you see I'm content? Leave me alone.* Sadly, nothing went away. There it all was in the shadows, waiting to jump out with the next attack. Desperation was setting in. I needed it to be out of my mind for good.

As I sat one day reminiscing over my teen years, I thought about the time I got so drunk, the time I went with my friends to two total strangers' apartment and drank to the point I cannot remember most of it. More than before, I realized how stupid it was of me. A wave of feeling foolish came over me as if it was happening again. I didn't like the feeling in the least.

Trying to understand why recalling this event was bothering me the way it was, I thought it through. I felt foolish because it was foolish. I couldn't change that fact. I could only learn from my mistakes. I didn't like it then, and even now the thought of how sick I was nauseated me. I justified that as a reminder to myself not to drink like that ever again—which I haven't. I worked through the feelings of embarrassment, immaturity, and disappointment in myself.

Then I reminded myself I still didn't remember all that happened that night. This is what was eating at me the most. I cringed and hated the fact that I had no idea what my actions, words, or thoughts were. I tried to play it off as just a drunken teenage night and just let it go. So often, we do something stupid or embarrassing and years later can look back and laugh at ourselves. Only this time I wasn't finding the humor. I had to ask myself why it was agitating me so much that I could not remember.

Several minutes went by and voilà! The answer came to me. I detested the fact that I did not have control. I had lost it. I had no control over how I acted or how others acted toward me. I had no control over my thoughts, decision-making, or the situation. Giving up my self-control had left me open for others to make choices for me. It was bad enough that I had been in the apartment of strangers. I would have never allowed it to go as far as getting into one of their cars. Either my friends or one of those guys had made the choice to put me in the car and push me out in front of my house. Of course, I was in no condition to make a decision for myself, but I didn't like that my rights had been removed from me. More so, I had given them up. It's my right to make my own choices, whether they are good or bad. I had made the choice to take the first drink. The alcohol had taken control of me and the situation. Lesson learned. I would never again allow something or someone to take my control. To this day, I have never drunk like that again. Admittedly, I do have a very rare drink on a special occasion. But I am in control and have prearranged transportation home if I am out.

In comparison, I realized this is why I did not like smoking marijuana. I had given up my control. I did not like the feeling of being powerless, and I had fought the high to keep my control. How could I ever mellow out if it was a battle of substance versus the human mind?

Comparing this lesson further to other areas of life, I looked at my childhood and being molested. I had no control over those events either. Nor did I have control over my brothers.

I was powerless over them.

My brothers controlled my every move and thought. There was no way I could be a normal kid when I was always trying to dodge them. As much as I tried my best to stay a step ahead of them, it didn't help because they had the power. How I slept was determined by them. I couldn't sleep soundly with both eyes shut. I was controlled and manipulated into thinking I was bad, guilty, and the cause of what was happening to me. This is similar to cases such as rape, spousal abuse, and kidnapping. These are comparable situations where the predator has to bring down his or her victim to achieve what it is he or she is after.

When the molesting finally stopped, the manipulation had planted its seeds in my mind. The roots spread and anchored themselves into my brain and soul. All the destructive feelings I had about myself grew deeper and larger. In time, not only did I believe these horrible things, I took them as gospel truth. For each time I said one of those negative things in my mind, it would take three times the amount of positive words or actions to combat it and make me believe differently. These seeds grew into weeds that blocked out all the beauty in my garden of life. These seeds were those bubbles that kept coming out and bringing me back down. I needed to be rid of them all so that I could enjoy what was beautiful around me, my family especially.

Discovering that all the control belonged to my brothers and I had none was the big bubble I had been waiting for, the one that finally burst and brought some good and helped me make some progress. It dawned on me that my brothers had had control all the years I was being molested. In a remote way, they still had it. This infuriated me. Just like my drunken night and pot-smoking days, I did not like my self-control being taken from me. It just wasn't fair.

I had no chance of getting control all those years ago, but by no means did I have to give it up now. I kept repeating to myself over and over, *They had control then, but it's done, and I want my control back.* I made the decision right there and then. I would control all the aftereffects from this point on. I was infuriated and determined. What made me so mad was all the time that had gone by that I could have lived by my own accord, not what was instilled by people who preyed on me. I wanted to live by my choices. I did not want to have to worry what others would think of me or find out about me. My teen years were wasted because I was in constant fear of people finding out the truth and it was instilled in me that I wasn't a good person or deserving of good.

For the first time, I was beyond angry over the past. Take any anger that I had in the past and triple it to understand how potent it was. I was mad, resented my brothers and what they did, but I had never been outright furious. It was as if I had venom running through my veins and

I was poised to bite. I was so livid, I wanted to scream. Damn it to hell, I was taking back what was mine. They chose how things went back then and took my childhood. It was now my turn to choose, and by no means would they inadvertently have a say in how this affected me ever again. My adulthood wouldn't be given up as easily as my childhood. I would control the situation from here on after. The ball was in my court, and I wasn't playing nice anymore.

If only I'd had my control back after the molesting stopped, my teen years, the years you discover your likes, wants, and needs, would have been more beneficial to me. But this wasn't how it was for me, and I didn't possess super powers to go back in time to change it. Instead, I spent them fighting myself and the memories. I had to accept that this enlightenment on control came when it was supposed to. I was where I was meant to be. Perhaps all those years ago, on that drunken night, I didn't listen to my inner voice and still went to that apartment because I was really supposed to ignore it. If I had listened, I wouldn't be learning and gaining the best from it now, when I needed it the most.

Every day after this insight, I repeated to myself and out loud, "They had control then. I have it now." Sometimes I would spend a length of time just saying it without prompting. Doing the dishes, cooking dinner, showering, no matter what I was doing, I would just repeat it over and over and over again. When a bubble would pop up in my mind, I broke it first and reminded myself I was in control. This was a challenge at first, but the more I said it, the more I had confidence in it and myself. The bubbles faded out in time. They didn't float away over-night, but they did disintegrate into thin air when one would surface because they lost their power over me.

Having this newfound tool freed my mind and my time to spend with my girls and husband.

Motherhood was filled with its own challenges, but still as breath-taking as I expected it to be. My girls had me 100 percent. No longer did I go through motions mindlessly, like a ghost. I could grasp things better when problems did arise, and I could appreciate and cherish mile-stones because I was more in tune and involved.

Simple everyday tasks could suddenly be completed in a suffi-cient amount of time. Before, something as simple as taking a shower could take me hours to complete. I would be distracted by the negative thoughts and try to counteract them by involving myself in another task. Now I gained focus and could think clearer than I had before.

Seeing what control gave me, I value it as one of my greatest achievements in my recovery.

Without it, I'd be stuck in the shell I was meandering through life in. It took a lot of patience, hope, and perseverance, but I am still proud that I regained control of my life.

CHAPTER 7

Confrontation

Some time went by after I took control. Busy raising my daughters along with my husband, life was treating us all well. The episodes of memories and flashbacks had lessened for me drastically. They were few and far between. Once in a while, I'd have to remind myself that I still had control and hadn't just dreamt it.

I really felt good about myself. My self-confidence was up, although it still needed some tweaking. My chin was up, and I smiled more often. I had more ambition than before. I was really looking forward to future events and the future in general.

Despite the fact that things had improved for me, I still had to encounter my brothers. Coming from such a large family, there was always some family event on the calendar: holidays, picnics, weddings, showers, baptisms, and birthdays. Having a vast number of nieces and nephews, there were many kid birthday parties. It was common for us to have gatherings on back-to-back weekends. There were also many weekends when there was more than one party to attend.

Before I took control, I hated going to family functions, because I felt awkward around my brothers. Even though none of them ever said a word or insinuated anything, I always felt humiliated and ashamed. Once I took control, I hated going because I held bitter feelings toward them. It was not easy seeing them all happy and having a good time. I would be in a corner somewhere wanting to scream, *How could you be having fun? Do you know what you did to me? Do you know what you took from me and what it cost?* Because my husband worked shift work, I attended most of the events alone with my daughters. This made it worse for me because I felt like I had no ally there for support.

With each event, I hesitated and was apprehensive about going to the next one even more so. The more I had to interact with my brothers, the more disgusted I became. I knew that, at some point, I would have to find a way to deal with this. If I didn't, there was a good chance of me blowing up in a rage at one or all of them in front of the entire family. I had imagined it hundreds of times over the years, and it wasn't a pretty scene. I always understood that if there ever was to be a confrontation or acknowledgement of the past, it would take place in a more private setting. Having a discussion with any of them related to the past was just something I imagined. I never considered the idea becoming a reality. There was no way. I plainly was not brave enough to handle that. Courage was not in my vocabulary.

Still, every time I turned around, another invitation arrived. Panic attacks set in occasionally just thinking about having to attend. If I had a legitimate reason to not go, I was thankful.

I never responded "no" just to get out of going. Besides, I was never good at lying, and if I tried to, I knew I'd be caught. I didn't need another issue on my plate, so I would just go. Especially if it was a kid's birthday party, I'd do it for my nieces and nephews. After all, they never did anything wrong and did not deserve to be slighted because of others' issues. My mother was another reason I would keep attending. I felt it would hurt her if I just didn't go and kept my daughters away also. In an odd way, I never wanted her to know the truth about what happened in her home and wanted to protect her.

Three months after the birth of my second daughter, I developed some symptoms and went to see our family practitioner. I had shortness of breath, heart palpitations, fatigue, and weakness with physical activity. Without hesitation, the doctor told me I had postpartum depression. Then changed his diagnosis to me being in a much deeper depression. He believed I was depressed because I couldn't have any more children. With my husband being the only male son, it would be the end of a family line. The doctor felt I was subconsciously under pressure because of this. I didn't agree in the slightest way. As much as I argued that it was not a concern of ours, he insisted he was exactly right. I was told to go home, relax, and enjoy the two kids I did have.

Two months later, I returned to the doctor because the symptoms worsened. He put me on an antidepressant. He was still insisting I was suffering some type of severe depression. I agreed to try the pills, but I still felt his diagnosis wasn't correct. Over the next several months, I went to appointment after appointment with no success. With each visit came more and more medication. When I demanded he run every kind of test possible, he would only give me the referral if I also went to see a psychologist. I was tired of him saying it was depression, and to prove him wrong, I went.

The psychologist I went to did the normal question-and-answer evaluation. In addition, she had me sit at a computer to answer another extensive series of questions. The next scheduled appointment, she gave me her findings and results. She found that I suffered from PMS and with that can come a very mild depression that would pass rather quickly. This type of depression would not have been happening for months like mine had. It's funny how I kept telling the family doctor that I wasn't suffering from serious depression and there had to be a physical diagnosis for the way I was feeling.

Back at the family doctor's, medical tests had pinpointed nothing so far. The doctor was unyielding in his diagnosis. I was told to continue with the psychologist. He didn't feel a proper assessment could be made in three visits.

I was tired of being physically ill and arguing with him. Desperate and almost to the point of a real depression, I scheduled more appointments with the psychologist. At least she seemed to listen to me. When I explained to her why I was back, she assured me my symptoms weren't just in my head and were not from depression. Being that the family doctor wasn't budging and my health insurance was paying, she asked if there was anything I would like her to assist me with.

In all the past years, I had never envisioned me going to a stranger for help with being molested. But spontaneously, I took her up on the offer. I told her what happened with my brothers, how I got through so far, and where I was at now in recovery. She was a little stunned that I had made progress on my own to that point. She praised my insight and said my thinking was very clear. She felt I had a good hold on my past. I told her about attending family functions and how the anger was eating at me. I was ready for the next big step. I needed to face my brothers, get answers, and move on. I just didn't know how to go about it. This is the help I asked the psychologist for.

Over the next two appointments together, we discussed my options. We played out the best- and worst-case scenarios with each suggestion. I could call each one and talk to them all individually. I could arrange a meeting with each or as a group. The phone seemed like a long, drawn-out process. Arranging meetings was out of the question. I was still afraid to face them. I had to get over that fear if I was to take this step. Any way we thought about, I also feared stumbling over my words. My confidence may have been up, but I still struggled with expressing myself verbally. I didn't want it to become a debate. Nor did I want it to become about them.

Listing what I wanted out of approaching them, I realized I wanted to say how I felt and what I needed to without interruption. After all, I had waited how long to utter a word? I deserved at least that much respect. I knew myself that if one of them stopped me midsentence or asked me to explain what I meant by something, I would shut down, end it, and not give it a second chance. I also realized the most important thing to me when going to my brothers was that I maintained control over the whole situation.

Another idea came to me. I could write one letter to all of them expressing everything I needed them to know and hear. The psychologist liked the idea. She had seen firsthand that I couldn't express in words what I wanted, but as soon as I had pen and paper, I could clarify beautifully what I was after. This option worked for me. I could speak through ink and paper exactly what I felt without interference. I wouldn't have to explain anything because I could explain everything as I wrote. Control was still mine, and they would all receive it by mail at the same time.

This is what was going to be best for me. People often ask why I chose this option. It's simple. I controlled the course of things now, and if my brothers didn't like it, oh well. They should have thought about it back then. I had a few concerns. One was their wives or children opening their mail. That was solved by certified registered mail. Only the recipient could sign for it or pick it up at the post office.

My other concerns were normal, like how would they react? Would it be over quickly? Would I regret doing it? And how was this going to impact others in the family once word spread? Would they deny or take credit? Would they contact me or ignore the letters? My psychologist helped me muddle through each image, question, and fear. She threw back at me more questions and suggestions of what may come. My response was the same repeatedly: they were all things I'd have to wait and see. For better or worse, I needed to write and mail the letters first. I would only be kicking myself later for not doing it and ceasing the opportunity of help.

On November 8, 1992, I sat for hours and wrote until my fingers were numb. Seven pages later, I was addressing envelopes. Before I mailed them out, I contacted my sister. I asked her to please come over; it was important. We sat down, and I told her everything. My sister was in a state of shock—surprised, but then again she wasn't. She said knowing the truth cleared up some questions about my behavior when I was much younger. She always wondered why I had such a hard time sleeping or would get upset when she wasn't going to be around. She cried with me, and I cried with her. She promised to support me through this. She fully agreed I needed to confront my three brothers. She had her concerns about mailing the letters, but understood why that was my choice.

It helped to know I had a second ally on my side. My husband had been with me already for years on this path. He never wavered and supported every choice I made. Having both my sister and husband there to hold me up helped diminish some of the fears I was having about the outcome. For instance, if any one of them ignored the letter or denied what they did, it was their problem, not mine. Same with if their wives or children found out, it was their issue to deal with, not mine. I always wondered if they told their wives previous to getting married as I had told my husband. I felt the need to take it upon myself and feel responsible if their lives were upset by all this. My sister and husband aided me in counteracting placing blame and guilt on myself. If they hadn't told their wives, shame was on them for entering into marriage without being fully honest. I would be sorry if trouble did come to others for my actions now, but I could not take fault.

I had no way of telling what the state of matter would be once those letters were out of my hand. I couldn't get them back, so anything else was possible. I just visualized a catastrophe starting once everyone got their mail. I was expecting screaming and yelling, name-calling, and insults. I anticipated nasty comments from my brothers, as well as their wives. If these were the results, I had to take them for what they were. Anger from many was probable.

No matter what occurred next, it took the backseat to me needing to have my say. In no way would I ever feel guilty for unburying what was bottled up inside of me almost my whole life. I was now twenty-seven and sick of dealing with what they did to me. Now was the time to let this all out so I could move on to something else in life. Up until this point, being molested, being a victim was what defined my life.

From somewhere inside of myself came bravery that I didn't really know I had. As nervous as I was, handing the letters over to the postmaster wasn't the bravest part. What was to follow was the courageous part. The letters all arrived to their destinations on a Saturday morning. It just so happens that all three of my brothers were home to sign for them. Immediately, they must have spoken with one another because by midafternoon my phone was ringing. My husband answered and handed it to me. He let me know it was my oldest brother. I wasn't expecting any response so quickly. This was my feat of bravery: taking the phone, listening, and speaking. My brother said everyone wanted to get together and talk and asked if I was open to sitting down with them. I agreed to do it the next night with the stipulation that it be at my house, my familiar territory. I hung up the phone and just dropped. My husband caught me and held me while I cried uncontrollably. I shook and trembled out of relief, pride, fear, and adrenalin.

Without even knowing I wanted it to take place, something I was waiting so long for was finally happening. Not so much the meeting and confrontation, but the wondering of how it could come about. When I daydreamed about facing them, it had always left me a bit disturbed. I would never have to imagine again what it would be like. It was becoming a reality.

The next day arrived. It was Sunday already, and I spent the day cleaning every nook and cranny in the house. My husband questioned me as to why I was making everything so nice for my brothers. I corrected him and informed him I wasn't cleaning for them. I was doing it for myself. Having my surroundings uncluttered and neat was beneficial for me to get through the meeting later on. It would help me think clearer and be more at ease. I wanted my setting to be perfect. After all, this was a big event that I had waited eons for.

By 7:00 p.m., I was ready as I ever would be. The first knock on the door came. I took a deep breath and let the first in. I wasn't nervous anymore. I was more anxious and had my guard up, ready to do battle if necessary. My husband was at my side, ready to assist and support me. Soon all three were there, and it was time to begin.

Afraid to look them straight in the eye at first, I didn't know exactly where to begin. Honestly, I had a lump in my throat the size of Texas. Luckily, one of my brothers broke the ice. He stated that everyone was surprised by my letters arriving and no one ever knew the past had such an effect on me. Because I never showed outward signs, they assumed I forgot, blocked it out, or moved on from it. My letter proved their thinking was on the wrong track.

Then the first question came: why did I mail a letter rather then just going to them and talking? Obviously, this wasn't the stereotypical approach. And apparently, each of their wives was home when the mailperson knocked on the door for their signatures. There was more confusion about my choice of contact rather than anger about it.

I gave them the easy answer first. It was best for me, and they weren't the main concern in my decision. I held my head high and looked directly at them, further explaining how I had tossed other options around with help of my psychologist. I let them know that, even now, with this finally happening, I would not give up an ounce of my control.

See, in the past, I would have backed down and taken the question as a personal attack. In the past, my normal reaction would have been to clam up, hold back my feelings, regret it, and then use the negative experience to beat myself up later. I shocked myself now because I clearly defended myself and stood my ground with them. I spoke from my heart. Although hard to believe, it felt good to me. My gut instinct was yelling out to roll with it. So, I did.

The remainder of the meeting became easier after that. We talked for three hours. There was a steady flow of questions, answers, and expressed feelings. I was given a lot of answers about the past and present. My biggest questions were why and did they remember. Surprisingly, not one voice was raised. There was no name-calling or shutting down of emotions.

One thing that was obvious was that they all remembered what they did. They didn't deny or ignore the facts as I suspected could have been a possibility. On the opposite hand, they had always wondered if I remembered. They all said they never approached me because they weren't sure. Also, they didn't know where I was at in my life. Bringing it up to me at the wrong time could have devastated me further and triggered more harm than good. So, in reality, they were looking out for me in the long run.

Each gave me his reason for molesting me. Ironically, each was completely different. Out of respect for their privacy, I will not divulge what motivated them to act out so violently. Each had personal issues that caused them to retaliate and take their anger, stress, and vengeance out on me. It was somewhat interesting to see how others' negative circumstances can cause destruction for innocent bystanders. Unfortunately, unaware of their situations, I happened to be easy prey, close by, to release their anger on.

There were apologies across the board. The words came from each of the three. One of my brothers, along with his apology, said, "I was the victim of circumstance." While that may have been true, the justi-fication was harsh to hear. In some manner, I felt his choice of words were a way of easing his guilt. So be it. If that is what he needed, then that was his emotional issue to handle, not mine. All I needed was the acknowledgement and apology.

If they could have gone back and changed time, they would have fixed this for me. One offered to help me continue with the therapist if I wanted to go further than the visits allotted by my insurance. I also had the offer of them going with me to group therapy if that was what I wanted. They said they would do whatever I needed them to do to get me through this and be happy. In return, they didn't demand anything from me. They just asked that I try my best to overcome what they caused.

I never did need anything from them after our confrontation. They did what was required once they knew what effect their actions held over me. Being honest, respectful, regretful, understanding, and aware were their obligations. My outcome was fortunate. It could have been a major disaster. Some victims who have made it to this point in recovery aren't so lucky. They have hostile confrontations filled with denial, disrespect, and accusations made against them. Whether confronting their molester or looking for support and revealing the hidden secret to a friend or family member, it can turn out negatively, leaving them feeling hopeless, demeaned, and unworthy.

I guess I envisioned the worst outcome for myself because, subconsciously, I was preparing myself for the aftermath that could have been reality. Realizing what were possibilities, I would not have been caught off guard and could control the level of severity. If I envisioned this confrontation through rose-colored glasses all along and it didn't come out that way, I don't think I could have survived the devastation.

Yes, their wives were upset and shocked. None of them had ever spoken to their wives about this before the letters arrived. I wouldn't have wanted to be a fly on any of their walls that day. The news did cause rifts amongst them as couples, but my brothers all understood that was their mistake and had to handle it. It wasn't for me to take blame for what they caused.

Their pasts had caught up with them, something they knew was a possibility on their side of the story. It just happened to come when they least expected it.

My sister helped me out and spoke to my parents. News spreads fast in large families, and inevitably they were bound to hear it through the grapevine. I didn't want them to hear it through the rumor mill. I certainly wanted them to hear it without prejudice and not through someone else's opinions. Not that I didn't want to tell them myself, but I was busy dealing with my brothers. My sister could tell them what I wanted, expressed without bias. She went before things got blown out of proportion. Also, we wanted to protect both my parents and wanted to show them respect by not letting them hear it as gossip.

Both my parents were hurt, disappointed, and in disbelief at first. My sister let them know about my letters and my meeting with my brothers. They couldn't understand how this had happened. And as I always thought true, they had no idea this was going on under their roof. They put a lot of blame on themselves as the parents. I later received an apology from them.

I didn't feel it was necessary for many reasons. I already understood they did the best they could for my siblings and me. I was sorry that they had to go through this. There was nothing I could do for them except assure them that I was okay. In the same sense, there was nothing they could do for me but understand. Time has eased their pain and rebuilt our family again.

Several weeks after our meeting, I returned to the psychologist's office. At the previous meeting, I had just started to think of what to say in a letter. Although surprised, she was proud that I had sent them and talked with my brothers. We talked about how I was feeling about the answers and details I had received. Having these things lifted so much weight off my shoulders, and I could now go on to better things. This was my last appointment with her. I accomplished what I needed her to help me with. I could go to family functions now and not have my past haunt me. The truth was out in the open, and I made a milestone in recovery.

Overall, taking the step of confrontation was successful for me. I have never doubted my decision to do so. I received answers to age-old questions. I was no longer a victim held hostage by memories. I had what I needed to move on in life. I could begin living without fear. I still had control over how things affected me. Now I had full control over my destiny too.

While all this was happening in my life, I still had the added problem of my health in general. I was waiting for answers in this area of my life also. I was still seeing the family practitioner almost weekly. About three months after I met with my brothers, I blacked out one day and suffered a loss of time. This is when things started coming clear medically. I also had a few dizzy spells. I assumed I had an inner ear infection because I had had several of them in my lifetime. The dizziness was normal, but the blackout was new. When I went to the doctor for him to check my ears, he didn't even check them. He pulled out his stethoscope and listened to my heart. There it was. He could hear a murmur.

I was referred out instantly to a cardiologist. An EKG and ultrasound showed I not only had a murmur, but also mitral valve prolapse, a common heart disorder. It occurs when the valve between your heart's left upper chamber and the left lower chamber doesn't close properly. The blackouts were resulting from too much oxygen to my brain. All the symptoms I had been suffering were also common with MVP. Finally, I had an answer. Even though I was in fear of dying from the symptoms, the actual condition was easily treated. Once I began medication, I was feeling more myself in a few months

Needless to say, I had all my records transferred to a new family practitioner rather quickly.

My old doctor had definitely made the wrong diagnosis. Actually, he jumped to a conclusion and claimed I had postpartum depression. I spent close to a year suffering and worrying needlessly. If he had just taken some time on the first visit to look into different possibilities, I may have been saved months of anguish.

Things always happen for a reason whether we like to admit it or not. My physician's bullheadedness delayed my physical diagnosis. While that is true, if he wasn't wrong and insisted I see the psychologist, I may not have searched out the support I needed from her.

Not having had that opportunity, I may not have confronted my brothers and gotten the answers I needed. Not sending those letters would have caused my mental suffering to linger longer. Worse than that, my recovery from the molestation could have been halted. Without doubt, the negative situation with my doctor resulted in a truly positive outcome that made my entire life better.

CHAPTER 8

Forgive and Forget (Well, Put Aside)

A lot came from within me to take the step of confrontation. It took every ounce of every quality and capability I had to follow through. If I had let all the doubt and fear hold me back, I would have missed out on the pot of gold at the end.

I purposely did not mention what the biggest outcome was from the letters and meeting. It is so big and incomprehensible to most that it deserves its own chapter. It was forgiveness, my golden reward.

Yes, I forgave my brothers, my molesters. Hell had finally frozen over. Some may not understand this in the least, but it was another choice that I chose to make. My only other option was to hang on to the damaging emotions. Resentment, disgust, hatred (of the act), betrayal, consumption, and hopelessness were all prominent. Odd as it may seem, even jealousy stuck its foot in the door. Most could never imagine this coming from being violated and abused. I have to admit that I was envious that my brothers seemed to be happy and content in life while I was stuck with the black clouds lying on my shoulders.

I had an addiction to all these bad qualities and feelings. Otherwise, I wouldn't have kept returning to them over and over throughout the years. This is all I knew how to be, and I was dependent on those feelings being there every day. My dependency on the negative was equal to that of a drug addict needing their fix each day. It was time for me to let them go and free myself from the darkness. This was part of why I chose to contact my brothers.

Sylvia Robinson, a famous singer, musician, and producer is responsible for the quote: "Some people think it's holding on that makes one strong. Sometimes it's letting go." I admire her words and understand them exactly. I was holding on to all the negativity, subconsciously thinking I was in some way beating the damage caused by being molested. By clinging to it, I wasn't letting my attackers get the best of me. My thinking was way off. I was causing myself to sink deeper into the hole. I was stunting my spiritual growth. This wasn't making me strong. It only proved all my weaknesses.

I felt drained and was worn out from fighting the battles within myself. I had to get a grip on my mental state. Granted, I had taken control over the situation, but my very own mental status was controlling me in return. At times, when a bad feeling brought me down, I would counteract it with sarcasm or make light of it. Holding in or deterring the emotions was not working anymore. So, when plan A doesn't work, resort to plan B.

Mahatma Gandhi once said, "The weak can never forgive. Forgiveness is the attribute of the strong." This is another quote that inspired me and brought light to my current state. He was correct. You do have to have strength to forgive. With each step I had taken in recovery up to the point of the confrontation, I had gained strength within. Without that strength, I could have never made it to the point of forgiveness. No other human could do it either. It's just not possible.

Plan B was the complete opposite of plan A. It was to forgive. Naturally, I could have switched over to plan B earlier along the road, but jumping to forgiveness too soon could have backfired later on. I'm sure if I had forgiven prematurely, emotions I possessed that were buried deep in my subconscious would have surfaced and bit me in the rear in the future. The time was right for my new course toward recovery. I had fully felt the pain from every possible hurt that molestation could have sparked off for me. I can't think of a rock I did not turn and beat myself up with. Not that I wanted to suffer longer than I had to, but I suspect any person would have to run the full process to move on and have it be successful.

Receiving the answers I needed at our meeting, I was able to understand many aspects. I clearly comprehended that I was not the weak one. I had survived all these years with the effects. It was my brothers who had the weakness to commit such an act. Although they had forces causing them to do so, they acted out and let their vulnerability take over. They knew their behavior was wrong, but still proceeded to hurt someone intentionally.

Almost as if I was getting the last laugh, I was proud that I didn't act out in any way that caused harm to others. All my revenge tactics had been aimed upon myself. If anyone was harmed by me, I did it without intent. All of this hit me instantaneously during our meeting. My opinions toward the past were changing as we spoke. Seeing the light and the view from the other side of the fence, I knew I'd be okay.

I could forgive my brothers for their weakness and poor judgment. In addition, forgiveness included not only molesting me, but the struggles caused as an after effect. It was what felt right. In a few hours' time, I was able to accept their apologies and let go of the past. To convey it in a few words is tough. It felt like many of the debilitating, nasty feelings I had for ages came to the top of my head and rushed out into the air. They were leaving in a hurry because they weren't necessary anymore. Forgiving what my brothers did didn't mean I was saying to them that what they did was okay. By far, the opposite. Their actions forced upon me were still as traumatic and abusive in my eyes. I forgave them for their actions, although I still believed no one should have ever suffered from such an ordeal.

Commonly, people who learn of my past ask how I could trust my brothers again. Let me clear up a lot of peoples' misconception. Trust and forgiveness are two different issues. In some instances, like mine, they can be interlinked. I do believe, without a certain amount of trust, forgiveness is ill-fated. But in reality, the two need to be handled separately. In some cases, it may take a long time to rebuild trust, or it may never happen. In my case, trust wasn't one of the bigger issues that weighed me down. Of course I did not trust my brothers all the years I was being molested. When it stopped, I didn't trust them out of fear there would be another time. At this point in time, numerous years had passed, and our only interaction was at family functions. We were all married with children and in many ways had gone our separate ways.

Never once was I alone with any one of them to tempt the Fates and see if they could be trusted. Not that I wanted to go there either. Frankly, I never gave trust much thought. I don't recall going through a process to rebuild trust. If I did, it was subconsciously, or all the other aftereffects were so prominent that I didn't realize I was doing it. It would be wrong of me to say that I did not trust them at the present time. They say time heals all wounds. Possibly. It worked on my behalf, out of view, to mend the mistrust I had for my brothers.

When it came to trust, I only had one thought come to mind. We always hear of repeat offenders who have more than one victim. We are told almost daily of serial predators. Though it is very possible, the media rarely report a one-time or one-victim offender. I needed to hear from them that I was the only one. This was not so my ego would get a boost from having sole rights. I wanted to trust that the molesting had stopped with me. It was important to me that they never acted out like this toward anyone else, especially their own children. Often I prayed to any higher power I knew of to intervene and not let this be the start of some vicious cycle. Their answers would affect whether I could ever consider forgiving them or have pity on them. I needed to ask each of them my question directly because they were three separate individuals. They did not commit violence against me as a group. There was no conspiracy. One did not know what the others were up to. This was revealed to me during our discussion. Hearing from each that I was the only one singled out told me they did not let their poor judgment and weakness go further. They did have a conscious and chose not to extend their mistakes to other innocent victims. I never pictured it going beyond me. Nor was I ever given any hint that it was happening elsewhere. Still, I had to ask for my data's sake.

I had to trust that their answers were honest and sincere, so I guess trust was part of our relationship. I'm just not sure whether it was there earlier or entered upon asking my question. Nothing in our talk previous to this led me to feel they were beating around the bush, being dishonest, or just saying things to appease me. I felt they were being very open with me. Being able to trust and feel all were being truthful allowed for me to continue on to forgiveness. If I felt their openness had any objective that was for their sole benefit or an ulterior motive,

I would not have been able to trust a word they were speaking. Nor could I go on to forgive them.

It was toward the end of our talk that I chose to forgive all three of them. At the time, I used few words. Most of my reasoning was held in my heart. Hours had gone by since our meeting first started, and I was becoming mentally drained. I just felt it best to keep it simple as to not complicate things.

Some people who find they need to forgive never come face-to-face with their offender. They hold what they would say verbally in their minds and souls. I was fortunate that I had the opportunity and that it wasn't a hostile scene. Others may see it important to stand right in front of their offender and say, "I forgive you." At times, this may backfire because the violator doesn't accept his guilt or see that he is a cause of the victim's problem.

If someone asked my advice, I would tell them this. Follow your heart. It's perfectly okay to keep what you would say to yourself. The important part is that you have found it within your soul to forgive. If you choose to confront your attacker, understand you may not be received with open arms. Also, be sure you realize it from all angles within your heart and mind before approaching. Beyond that, if you are confident that saying, "I forgive you," to your wrongdoer will bring you closure so that you can move on, then go for it.

My intentions for approaching my brothers were never to leave them with any type of hurt.

Although I was the priority, everyone needed this to be resolved. It was for all of us and the family's sake as well as future generations. I could have just dumped everything on my brothers and walked away. That would have created a larger void that had to be conquered. Without resolution, no one was going to gain from this. Getting it all out in the open so that forgiveness could come about was the only way functional relationships could happen. I had had enough and needed to forgive them to function as an individual.

Growing up, we were distanced from my father's family. The separation was caused by a conflict over borrowed money between my father and one of his brothers. Compared to molestation, it's stupid and minor. But that's the family legacy we are all left with. My dad's family was twice the size of mine, and everyone chose sides. No one could let go of the grudges and ill feelings. They missed out on many memorable things that should have been shared amongst family. I never got to know any of them because of issues they chose not to deal with in an adult manner. When there was an occasional invitation to a wedding or such, my younger brother and I were excluded due to the age limit of guests. This further removed them from my life. Many of my father's siblings have gone to the grave, and never has an apology been spoken. No one ever forgave anyone either. This always bothered me, and I still find it so sad. I certainly did not want the same for my siblings and me. And in the same aspect, I didn't want my girls to miss out on getting to know their aunts, uncles, and cousins.

Extending forgiveness to any type of offender does not mean you have to continue on in a relationship with him or her. It happens relatively often where someone will forgive but opt to have no future contact with their wrongdoer. In other circumstances, victim-offender relationships become and remain very neutral once all the laundry is aired and wrongs are forgiven. There's no anger, and on the opposite side, there's no love or caring feelings. Then there are situations like mine, where the victim wishes to continue the relationship afterward.

Luckily, things worked out as I had intended. As I said previously, I approached my brothers for my sake, as well as the family's benefit. I had every intention to continue contact with my brothers. This is the way it had to be. No matter what came about from the meeting, we all shared the same parents, siblings, aunts, uncles, and so on. Without doubt there were going to be events and holidays. Considering breaking off ties with them would have caused further grief and was an unthinkable option. The last thing I ever hoped for was to be distanced as my father's family was. I assumed if I did not forgive my brothers, the air would have still been a bit dense when at gatherings with them. I would have been okay being around them, but unfinished business would have still lingered in the air. Choosing to find forgiveness cleared all restraints. I gained the family I already had. No longer did I feel like the wallflower. I could attend these events without anxiety, anger, and interference from the past. Holding conversations with relatives and learning their likes and dislikes was new to me. I had avoided many of them before, or my full attention hadn't been on our conversations. I was so cooped up that most of what people said to me went in one ear and out the other. They were all the same people they had been before, but it was like meeting for the first time.

As soon as I put forth forgiveness, a wave of freedom washed over me. I would always be tied to my past, but I would never again be tied down by it. To forgive doesn't mean we forget what was done. You probably never will forget what happened. Perhaps it's best not to. We'd be losing a big part of ourselves. Through forgiveness, we can remember without all the emotional issues linked to it. I may have awarded my brothers by granting them forgiveness, but it was my reward in the end.

Forgiveness, much like love, respect, and innocence, comes from our souls, not our minds.

Equally, they are all hard to define in basic words. Our egos allow us to hold on to grudges and all the harmful and restrictive feelings created by another person. To be able to forgive, we have to work from our soul. When we release the past and all the baggage that comes with it, we make room for our soul to take the forefront. Not until then can we gain the healing benefits of forgiveness.

Even with an apology from the other person, just accepting it is not enough. We're responsible for letting go of the pain in order for forgiveness to come about. This was something I realized at a young age, I had to deal with the feelings that were impacting me. No one or no thing could remove them or take them away for me. Blame belonged to my molesters for creating the opportunity for me to develop these feelings, but it was my responsibility to change or resign them. It took me a long time, but I was doing it my way, on my own, and only going after what I could handle each step of the way.

By letting go, I opened myself to a whole new world. By being able to forgive, I felt like I matured immensely. I was no longer the frightened little child afraid of the scary, evil monsters under my bed. It was so freeing. My life was full of opportunities now. Nothing was holding me back from getting out there and exploring. I grew spiritually and morally. The black shadows that surrounded me had changed to pure white light. My mind was at peace, and my thinking was much more focused. Physically, I had energy and was up and moving about spontaneously. As I awoke each morning, I was anxious to see what would inspire me that day. I could take the time to appreciate little things in life more. Before, I was so often distracted by old haunts and feelings that it left me little time for other, more important, things.

The feature that makes us stand out from others often causes us the most pain in life. This can be a physical feature, personality trait, or an emotional or mental issue. These are just some examples of how one can stand out amongst his or her circle. The unusual, hidden, or odd component is what usually brings us challenge and obstacles in life. It also isolates us and prevents further growth until we come to terms with it. Surely, being molested was the part of me that was hidden and odd and caused many obstacles for me. Not until I accepted and dealt with the abuse, and forgave my brothers did I truly begin to grow. By forgiving, I was able to accept that being molested was a part of me and I had to respect it as much as I disliked it.

How many times have we all heard to forgive and forget? It's bluntly stated as if the two parts are one in unity. I don't know about anyone else, but I must have missed the invitation to their marriage in the mail. All sarcasm aside, my point is they are two distinct things. To partner them together does the first of the two an injustice. Forgiveness is the act of letting go. It is as much a mental as spiritual means of ending all anger, resentment, and bitterness caused by an offense committed toward you by another person. As part of this, one cannot expect the person to be punished or pay compensation.

Forgetting, on the other hand, is like pushing back memories of a wrong committed against you by another. It is referred to as repression in the mental sense. When memories and emotions are repressed, they become reserved. They are more or less saved so that they can be brought back around at a later time. Looking at it from this view, to forget contradicts to forgive.

Forgetting can also be taken as removing and never recalling again. First of all, I can't even fathom that never remembering is possible. Secondly, removing them, in my opinion, would be like denial. Why would I want to work through so many issues just to turn around and deny them? Good or bad, feelings, situations, and other people are all tools that help us grow as solid human beings. They are like yucky vegetables. We don't much like them, but we have to eat them to establish healthy growth.

That is why this chapter's title ends with "(Well, Put Aside)." I don't like or agree with the standard notion of forgetting. Setting the past aside suits my outlook much better. Notice I do not put it behind me. That would only prevent me from ever looking back. The past and everything I had gone through is still with me. I have set them aside of me as if on a shelf to look at as nostalgia. They are there for me to look upon and remember the lessons I have learned from each. A teacher taught me my ABC's and how to read, and those lessons and skills gained are instilled in me for life. Well, just like that, the knowledge and skills I gained from being molested will always be with me. I can refer back to a math text-book and see how I solved an arithmetic problem. In the same sense, I can refer back to previous chapters of my life and see how I coped and resolved an issue such as humiliation or anger. The skills we need to lead fulfilling lives come from all sorts of teachers. To forget my past would mean all my struggles were for no purpose and a complete waste of time.

Achieving forgiveness reminds me of "The Butterfly Story." I would love to give credit for this enlightening tale, but I'm sorry to say the author is unknown. The story tells about the challenges of a butterfly's metamorphosis. A man finds a cocoon, and one day a small opening appears. He watches it struggle as it tries to emerge from the little hole in its casing. The man decides to help the creature and removes the cocoon, allowing it to emerge prematurely. The butterfly is loose, but deformed and unable to fly. This is how the butterfly spends the rest of his life.

By the man making it easier, the butterfly missed out on a required struggle that was crucial for his wings to develop fully. Being handed his freedom rather than earning it and not completing the change properly, the butterfly was denied of its beauty and entire potential.

At times struggles are necessary and valuable to our lives. God allows us these tests so that we won't be stifled. What would be the purpose if we went through life with no obstacles and lessons? Pretty boring, I think. We would never grow or learn and never develop wings that let us fly.

Struggling is exactly what I did to leap into and beyond each step in my recovery. Forgiveness was the final step that freed me. Without it, my wings would not have finished forming. I would have never been able to spread them and fly.

CHAPTER 9

Freedom to Do for Others

In a few weeks' time, things settled down after facing my brothers. It took that long for it to sink in exactly what had happened. The morning after, I awoke thinking perhaps I had dreamt it all. Stumbling into the living room bleary-eyed and seeing the kitchen chairs I had set up for extra seats still there from the previous night proved it must have really happened. Knowing it happened in reality didn't deter me from saying, "Wow!" every time I thought about it.

Even today I say the same thing. I actually did it. Once the initial honeymoon phase passed, I was left with time not burdened by past history. The liberating feeling was almost indescribable. To not have that constant cloudiness and negativity really gave me a new sense of independence. As much as I had freedom, I also gained a void that needed to be filled. I wasn't that victim looking for answers and obsessed with hope anymore. I needed to seal the gap with another part of me or a new one.

I spent a lot of my time with my daughters, raising and nurturing them. At that time I was also working part-time at a local retail store for minimum wage. It was to my advantage that I did not need a sitter—the girls could come to work with me for a few hours until my husband was done with his shift. Juggling work and motherhood had its challenges, but it always seemed to work out in the wash. I truly enjoyed having my time outside the home and interacting with the public, but I knew I didn't want be a store clerk forever ordering supplies and stocking shelves. I also cherished my free time. I worked on my crafts, read, gardened, and baked.

My wish was to finally go to college to advance myself. Enrolling for a course or two to improve my resume would have made me happy. It had to wait. I promised my girls would always come first. Besides, financially we could not accommodate the tuition in our budget. Although I had freedom unlike before, I still could not jump up and follow all my dreams at once. Responsibility took precedence over fantasy. That didn't mean I had to stop dreaming. I just had to put some personal stuff on the back burner until the timing was right.

In the past, anytime I did fantasize about becoming something or someone in the career sense, the feelings of inadequacy and unworthiness prevented me from reaching out to make anything reality. Now with the freedom to dream and choose a career path, I had a few obstacles to overcome. I had to accept that seeking the education needed to achieve any of the occupations I was pondering wasn't in the cards for me yet.

Having my freedom gave me the liberty to envision all the things I did not dare dream before.

I never gave what I could be much thought. If a genie had popped out of a bottle and granted me one wish to become whatever I wanted to be, I would have wished to instantly be turned into an elementary school teacher. The idea of inspiring children and being a positive influence in their development had immense appeal to me. It would be an honor that other parents put their children in my hands each day to play a key role in their lives.

In what seemed like a blink of an eye, it was time for my oldest to start school. Kindergarten, ready or not, here we come. She had a whole new world to explore and learn in. A new door opened for me also. It wasn't long before I was volunteering for ice cream socials and other school activities. I made new friends just as my daughter was making them. Although the PTA ended up being a huge, snobbish social clique that didn't welcome newcomers with open arms, I still wanted to be involved with my daughter's schooling.

As parents together, my husband and I made the choice to transfer our daughter to the Catholic school in our community. My husband had grown up in this parish and was an alumnus of the school itself. He was all gung ho for the change. On the other hand, I was looking at the long term for our little student. There appeared to be more of an educational structure, which would prove to be beneficial in later years.

Our daughter adapted and did extremely well. I excelled right along with her. Not being eligible for government funding as the public schools are, the professional staff was very appreciative of any volunteer time offered. Both my husband and I became lunch parents, monitoring the students during their meal and recess. Once word got out through the grapevine of my creativity and imagination, I became a household name, or rather a schoolhouse name. Teachers and parents would approach me seeking help with this and that.

My daughter was of the age where she needed an activity outside of school and home. A friend suggested I enroll her in a well-known girls' club one night a week along with her daughter. I made a few calls and signed her up. It wasn't long before the leader was coming to me for craft ideas and use of my time and hand. That's the thing with tiny small towns; all things are connected, and news spreads fast.

About once a month, I would go to the meetings and share my creativity with the girls. I loved it. To be able to mentor and guide these little bundles of energy was a privilege. I was always impressed that everyone's completed craft came out so different than the sample I made. Each girl found some way to make her project unique and individual to her taste and personality. I truly felt at home when at meetings. Equally, my daughter loved when I could be there with her.

The group leader was retiring after thirty-some years of holding the position. No one wanted to try to fill her shoes. In time, the position was offered to me. There were things I had to consider before giving a reply. One was childcare for my youngest while at meetings and on field trips. Second thought, just how much time would be consumed taking this on? I was still working part-time, volunteering at the school when needed, tending to a three-year-old and a first grader, and fitting my husband in somewhere. My real concern was my ability to handle everything I was taking on.

With some debate, I made the decision to take over the position of group leader. Yes, it was going to take hours of planning, attending meetings, and trips. If I was going to make this move, I had to have full dedication. I would be taking on an obligation in which many people and children depended on me. The pro that swayed me to say yes was the fact that this was a form of being that schoolteacher I wished to be. Going back to school and earning a degree still wasn't financially available. I rationalized that becoming a leader/mentor would suffice and be a step toward my very long-term goal. The position would fulfill all my needs of needing to be someone—but without the paycheck. In my heart, I knew I could do an excellent job. Down the road, this would be potential experience to submit on a resume.

I took on the challenge and surpassed all required expectations. More than being organized, time management played a key role in juggling home and volunteer duties. Children learn by what they hear and see. To teach them properly, I had to be a good example and live by the group's code of ethics. I so strongly believed in the values contained in the code that it became a way of life for me and my family also Today, I still agree with these standards and will for the rest of my life. Even my husband signed up to be one of my assistants. I have a talent for using my resources, and if there was something my group of "girls" needed, I found a way to get it. From crafts, trips, guest speakers, and supplies, I always found the way to make our plans work out and become reality. Often, other groups would hear of our many successful endeavors and borrow our information and ideas. Not much time passed before other leaders were turning to me for advice and guidance. It brought a ray of sunshine to my life to help others and see them reach their goals also. Doing what I was doing came easily and naturally because it was always from my heart.

As my "girls" grew, so did I. Being that I was never permitted to join any clubs or after-school activities, I had never had an experience like this. In many ways, I was regaining the youth I had missed out on. Everything I did with my "girls" was new to me. In my parents' home, growing up, little girls were to be little ladies, playing with dolls and wearing dresses all the time. Little girls were never supposed to be out getting dirty, camping, hiking, painting, and visiting local firehouses to climb on the trucks. Becoming a leader allowed me the rebellion to go against that stereotype. Don't get me wrong; the girls still had to wear dresses on occasion and plan a tea party here and there. But as their leader, I showed them the world was open to them and they could be whatever they wanted to be.

No one had really come to me for counseling and guidance before. In the rare instance that someone would ask for my opinion, I could never fully trust that they didn't have an ulterior agenda and would use it against me in some way. For the first time in life, I had the admiration of other adults and small children. I could feel myself shining. I felt this is where I was to be on my path of life. I was aware of my capabilities and had the inner confidence to use them. Most of all, I could put trust and faith in my associates that they truly respected my opinions. On the other hand, I placed my admiration on all these new women in my life because they were role models and examples to other adults and girls alike. I looked to them and followed their ways to improve upon my weaknesses.

Years went by. Both my daughters were in elementary school and developing and thriving well. Naturally, I signed my youngest daughter up to join "the group" as soon as she was of age. She enjoyed it as much as her older sister. In addition to leading my "girls," I was active in recruiting and training new leaders. I became a designated mentor of other leaders in various age groups. I also chaired many event and program committees. My personal group always retained a membership of sixteen to twenty girls. Overall, membership throughout our community soared to levels it hadn't been at in years. Word of all the wonderful programs and new dedicated leaders who were recruited was spreading like wildfire.

Soon I took on an even bigger role while still holding my other titled positions. I became our area manager. Under my watch were another twenty-some groups that I oversaw in addition to my own. I was responsible for making sure other adult members received appropriate trainings and the program was being delivered properly and safely. I worked closely with our board of staff as spokesperson for our area and, in turn, reported findings and statistics to our national headquarters. My date book was filled with meetings and activities. It was an immense and tedious job that required much more of my time.

The only thing that allowed me the extra time to take my newest position was the fact that I had been laid off from my part-time job. Otherwise, my plate would have been overly full and volunteering would have become a burden at the time. I didn't have to hurry out and find another job with a paycheck. Although college still wasn't a budgetable option, financially, we were stable enough that my few dollars a week wouldn't put us in a deficit. This allowed me to dig myself deeper and deeper into the organization. I would have found it hard to handle my many responsibilities without the support of my husband. He came to my aid whenever I called upon him.

All seemed to be going well, but gradually as time passed, I was overwhelmed and torn between my group and requests from my council superiors. My duties as manager were pulling me away from my "girls." The council started putting weight on me and other volunteers to increase membership numbers. Their priorities were numbers, racial image, and funding. Not that this isn't a good thing, but after a certain amount of time, I believed that quality over quantity was necessary. We could have recruited lots of new members, but without quality leadership, we would lose those new additions, plus old ones. There comes a time when you have to work with what you have and aim to build that to its best potential. My superiors kept pushing the enrollment issue to meet the demographics and race percentages of our community. They forgot to congratulate us on the fact that we did have the first bilingual Hispanic and Latino group in our neighborhood, which had a terrific bilingual leader who was running a fabulous program. Yet, according to demographics, we should have had three Asian girls registered as members. They constantly urged us to keep going out and trying to find these girls and enroll them. Most all of our volunteers in our area played dual rolls as leader and committee members. I was the rare case who did not work in addition to raising a family. Our women volunteers were struggling between maintaining their own groups and recruiting to meet our council's goals. The same dilemma was weighing on my shoulders.

I argued the point over and over again to no avail. My first and foremost obligation was to my "girls." I had gotten involved with this organization to be a mentor and teacher, not to be out on scavenger hunts for the paid higher-ups. I was becoming very aggravated with all the behind-the-scene things I was learning about.

With all the titles I was endowed with, more and more of my time was being taken from my family. Easily I was putting in forty-plus hours a week to accommodate my "girls" and my superiors. Seventy-five percent of my volunteer work was being done at home. It became habit for me not to change out of pajamas all day long and not bathe until it was time to attend a scheduled meeting for my group or for the council. I was literally becoming a hermit. I was being taken advantage of in more ways than one. Due to the fact that I did not work outside the home, I was always the one called on to handle everything. I often heard, *"Well, you're home all day, and no one else is."* I was being treated like crap, to put it bluntly.

Requests turned into demands. Staff stopped asking me if I could do something. I was receiving e-mails and phone calls with phrases such as "You have to…" and "Be here…"

I was being made to feel like dirt beneath their feet, and I was their doormat. I was sinking into a depression over this and believing the feelings I had inside me were really what I was.

It got so bad that it was time to make some choices.

Basing my decision morally on the fact that I needed to make a difference to my fifteen or so girls rather than on a national level, I stepped down from position of manager after three years. I just couldn't do it anymore. I felt I was being disrespected, and as much as I expressed my concerns, those in higher positions did not have the time or intention of hearing me. I continued with my group, as these girls were in their teens now and needed a positive influence in their life outside of school and home. I adored each and every one of them. I kept them under my wing and encouraged them to reach out for the stars. One of the added benefits to this was my husband and I got to share many memorable experiences with our daughters as well as their friends.

I was back on track with my "girls" and still held some of my other positions on the local area level. I not only enjoyed still planning events, but my "girls" were old enough to come up with their own ideas and handle some of the planning. I was proud of them. It showed me that I had brought them up through the ranks properly and helped them grow into young adults. They were proud of themselves when they could see their own success. I am happy to say most all of my "girls" have gone on to be successful and responsible adults.

As for me personally, I had sunk into a hole of depression. A bad taste for volunteering was in my mouth. Not that my "girls" weren't wonderful, but I had run the full course with them.

In another year or so, they would all be graduating high school and moving on. Most of the women I had developed friendships with over the years had moved on and resigned because they lacked support from our board of paid staff and were burnt out. It was sad to see this extended family drifting apart and going their separate ways. Even though I wasn't in a position to be at odds with the council anymore, my experience with these superiors damaged my outlook on the organization and their goals. Unfortunately, negativity had crept in and was slowly bringing my volunteer years to an end.

On the home front, my daughters were grown. My oldest was going to be sweet sixteen, and the younger had reached the teen years at thirteen. Neither needed me much anymore. They both had their social lives and school. It appeared that they both held the attitude that it wasn't cool to hang with a parent or chat with one either. My daughters weren't as dependent on me as they were in the past, except when it came to transportation. Quite frequently the words "Take me to the mall," "Take me to so and so's," and "Pick me up at…" came out of their mouths. Just as often, they both needed to be places at the same time in opposite directions. It seemed as I had been down sized to a mere chauffeur. Oh, and how I hated driving!

My daughters' requests for rides back and forth got abusive. I was expected to pick up and drop off numerous friends too. It seemed as if I was the only parent who drove or had a van to hold them all. If I put my foot down and said no because I wanted a night off or time to myself, I was inundated with the whiny, snippy teenage attitude. Keeping them home proved several times to be more punishment to me than them. Either way, I suffered and paid the consequences. I felt belittled and a failure as a parent.

Overall when it came to parenting, I was having trouble coping with the pre-empty-nest syndrome. As I stated, my girls just did not rely on me like they previously had. They had been a large part of my identity for years, and I was feeling lost. I didn't know how to let go of mothering someone at all times. It wasn't their intention, but I took it as being pushed away and rejected. None of this helped the depression that was rampaging and rooting itself within me more each day.

Sad and lonely, I waited each day for some big sign that would change my mood. It never came. My girls were certainly big enough to get themselves off to school every day. This allowed me to stay in bed. I started avoiding meetings because I had no desire to go out of the house. My house was my safe zone where no one could see exactly how low I had really become. If I did go out, I was sure to put on my full makeup and dress decently. It was like putting on a mask or costume to cover up the real me. Soon, I ignored the phone. I just did not feel like talking. No one ever called to see what I needed or how I was. The person on the other end wanted a favor from me or needed me to fix a problem. The same applied to e-mails. When I couldn't be reached by phone, they had a backup. The feeling of being used and abused was tearing me apart inside. So much for freedom, I was always bending to do for others and very little for myself. I was trapped in a cage of service to others.

Making matters worse was my sudden fear of driving. This was a complication as big an issue as the depression. I had driven for years. It was common for me to leave a note for my husband letting him know I had gone on a road trip with the kids to visit my friend ninety miles north or was going out shopping for the day. Out of the blue one day, I just went into a panic attack on the way to the grocery store two miles from home. A few more attacks followed while driving. The worst of them had me arguing with myself out loud and left me numb on my whole left side. I made the dangerous decision to make a U-turn in the southbound lanes of a highway, go against traffic, and head back north to the nearest exit to get me off the highway. After that, I limited my driving to the least amount possible, keeping me further trapped in the house.

This only caused me to go into anxiety attacks anytime someone asked me to give them a ride. Being the good person I am, I covered up my stress so the asker wouldn't feel like they were being an inconvenience. Holding in the apprehension was not good for me at all. Ironically, I could get in the car and be okay if I had someone riding with me. Even if it was one of the kids, I felt secure. If I was driving somewhere alone, the panic set in only on the way to my destination. Once I was headed home on my return trip, I was calm and fear-free.

From the fear of driving, I developed the skill of procrastinating. I could always go to the store tomorrow. I made every appointment I could for times that my husband would be off work. When the time came, I'd get him to come along with me for company, then make an excuse so he would drive also. I hid this fear from him as much as I possibly could. Inside, I knew I needed to seek help for this, but with all the other things I was feeling, I kept ignoring it and making excuses.

I lost trust in just about everyone. I suspected anyone who came near me was going to take something else from me. I wanted to be left alone to be me. If I could have locked myself in a closet and not come out until I felt something good was going to happen for me, the moths would have eaten me alive first. There was no light at the end of the tunnel for me to know that better days were ahead.

My world was glum and dreary. I was constantly on edge in anticipation of the next kid needing a ride or the next person who needed another favor. The anxiety had taken over to the point I would just sit and shake. My nerves were like little fragile china dolls teetering on a shelf. I could not focus on as much as a comic strip in the Sunday funnies. Thoughts raced in and out of my head faster than I could finish thinking the first one. My head was spinning like a top. Things had gotten so bad for me that I just wanted to go back to bed and stay there. It was perfectly okay with me if I went to sleep and never woke up. Perhaps that would put an end to my misery.

In my eyes, I was a complete failure and a train wreck. I had no clue how I had gotten like this. After all, I was always being nice to people. Never did it seem that others did nice things for me in return. I started to believe that if I were no longer here on this earth, no one would miss me. They would only miss the things I did for them. I was home all the time at their beck and call. After all, I did not have a real job. Therefore I was just a "nobody," so I may as well just make other people happy. Apparently, there's some rule that says nobodies don't deserve to be happy.

None of these bad feelings were just idle thoughts. I had said them to myself so many times that I accepted them as the truth. I felt worthless and a burden to my husband. As much as I attempted to make myself feel better, I couldn't escape. If I made plans to do something for myself that ensured a simple change of scenery outside the house, something came up that deterred my plans. I was doomed to be nothing and nobody. I gave up all hope of ever being someone, and happier times, forever.

My husband watched closely for months as I got worse. He didn't know how to talk to me about it. I always took it as being under personal attack when he spoke to me. Actually, he wasn't berating me. Nor was he babying me either, which is what I was looking for in an odd sort of way. This was all new to him too. He was trying to listen to my problems and give me the simplest answers possible not to upset me further. The depression caused me to be over the limit when it came to sensitivity. In another sense, he knew I had to ask for help first. Forcing it could make matters, or me, worse. He was just waiting for the day when I was ready. When I tried to talk to him about it, his advice was to do something about it. That was just it; I had no concept of how to change what was happening to me. At other times, he told me to look for a job or find something to do outside of the house. He didn't realize it, but this hurt me even further. It was bad enough other people looked down on me because I did not have a real, paying job. It made it worse to think my husband felt the same way. Later on, I would find out he didn't intend for me to take it that way. He understood how crucial my volunteer work with the girls' organization was for me and how important it was to me to be making a difference in the lives of these young girls. What I was gaining from volunteering far outweighed the benefits from a paycheck. Unfortunately, it had taken its toll on my mental health.

I had already crawled under a rock and felt like I was destined to remain there. If someone called my name, I would have looked around and asked who that was. I lost all identity with myself. I didn't recognize my own reflection in the mirror. I was just a walking, breathing shell inside a bubble who somehow awoke each day but found it difficult to sleep at night. Insomnia was the pits. I rarely showered anymore. With no appetite, I was losing weight and getting weaker physically. I stayed in the same pajamas morning, noon, and night for days at a time. It did nothing for me but allowed me more time for negative self-talk. None of that talking ever made sense either. I'd stop halfway through a sentence and finish it with the last half of the next racing thought. It may not have been so bad if I had some energy with the insomnia. At least then, I could have been up all night cleaning and doing laundry, which I had no strength for during the day. My house was a pigsty. I had let it go for a long time. My intuition was telling me I couldn't fight the depression anymore. I just wanted to give up.

I also knew enough that if I didn't seek help professionally, one of the next steps would be to start thinking suicide. I didn't want to die in reality, just felt like that. I was withering away to nothing and wanted to prevent the next drastic stage. I was awoken one night by the phone ringing at 12:30 a.m. It happened to be a wrong number, but my nerves were shot, and it sent me into a full-blown panic attack, shaking uncontrollably and sweating profusely. It took every ounce of strength I had to focus and keep the phone still to dial. My husband was on the night shift. Although my words were coming out garbled and scrambled, he got the clear picture that I needed him home. It only took him seven minutes to make it to our house. For that short amount of time, all I could do to keep myself from losing it completely was to sit on our couch rocking back and forth while humming.

It seemed like an eternity before he came through the front door. When I saw him, all I could do was look at him bug-eyed. No noise came out of my mouth when I tried to talk. I began to cry, and he grabbed me and held me until I was calm enough to finally say something. My exact words were, *"It's time. I need help."* My hero, he knew what I meant without further explanation. I passed out from exhaustion in his arms.

First thing in the morning, which happened to be a Sunday, we made the necessary calls to our primary care doctor and insurance carrier. Even at my lowest state, I was determined to keep control for myself. I did not feel I'd get the proper care I was looking for at the local ER. I wanted to go straight to a mental health facility that would start getting to the root of my problems the minute I walked in the door. I wanted a one-shot deal and not the frustration of a bunch of needless physical tests. Don't know how I managed it, but I was able to express this to the insurance representative and my doctor on the phone. More baffling, they agreed with me and gave me the approval to bypass the local ER trip.

My husband drove and stayed by my side all day until a room was found for me late that night. I was scared, but I knew in my heart that I was making the right choice. This was the first time in an extremely long time that something felt right to me. I didn't want to feel horrible anymore.

I had seen many nurses, interns, and psychologists in the mental facility's intake department. Every one of them asked if I was suicidal. They all got the same answer: "No, but if I don't get help, I will be." The next question was could I hurt myself. I knew I had to be honest if I wanted help from these people. So, I gave them the truth. I didn't know if I could hurt myself. Then again, I never thought I'd be this depressed and having a nervous breakdown, so their guess was as good as mine.

Without fail, each and every one needed a family history as well as a sexual history. The topic of being molested had to come up. Over and over again, I had to explain to them I was over that. Still not believing me, they would delve for more information. I would rattle off each step I took to overcome the battle. In return I'd get from them a confused "Oh" or "Okay." I still, even today, can't comprehend professionals who can't grasp that there are victims out there who are living as survivors and are not consumed, consciously or subconsciously, about their past trauma.

Now that they had every piece of info on me that they could possibly want, they couldn't understand why I was so depressed. They offered me to leave with a sedative and head home. Or if I felt I needed to stay, I could. Of course I stayed and admitted myself voluntarily. I didn't intend to go home only to have to come back. Or in the worst-case scenario, go home, become more depressed, causing me to become suicidal. I intended to get to the bottom of this depression. I wanted to be alive again. So a new chapter in my life was to begin.

CHAPTER 10

Behind the Mask

My stay in the mental facility wasn't all that long. Four days, to be exact. The first day was mostly spent in the ER due to a bed shortage. They found me a bed on the wing for anorexic teens until a proper one become available. I remained on that wing until late the next afternoon when a room was found for me on the wing for women's issues. My treatment there for depression lasted only three days.

According to my insurance carrier, I had a husband who was a willing support system for me, and he could take me home and care for me there. The only way my caseworkers could negotiate even another half-day stay was if I were suicidal or a threat to someone else. They get you one way or another. In actuality, even though their reasoning ticked me off a bit, I was glad to go home. As much as the stay did me good, it freaked me out in other ways.

I had never been exposed to this type of environment before. The women's wing consisted of the depressed, the addicts, the suicidal, the psychotic, and the homicidal. I earned the nickname Mary, as in the Virgin Mary, because I was the only first-timer out of the forty or so patients and therefore a virgin. Then there were girls so doped up on meds, they didn't even know they had a name.

The ones who made me physically ill to my stomach were the ones who stood around on free time comparing battle wounds from attempted suicides. The endless debate was to cut vertically, horizontally, or a little of both. They would be arguing over who had the better scar from where they slit their wrist. Of course, somebody's was always better. Then the dialogue would go something like this: "Oh yeah? I got one better. When my third attempt didn't work, I tried it this way." And they would literally shove their scarred wrists and arms in your face. I was rather naive on the subject. To be honest, it all freaked me out a bit.

The one who that frightened me out of my booties was the psychotic women next door to my room who first tried drowning herself in her shower. She failed, but managed to flood her entire room. The water flowed into my room and her adjacent neighbor's on the opposite side. Next, she broke into my room twice while I was meeting with the doctor and ransacked it. Although the nurses assured me she wouldn't sneak out again, I wasn't comfortable sleeping with both eyes shut at night. Lights out at 11 p.m. was enforced literally. There was not even a dull glimmer of light I could count on for security or protection.

When the intercom would boom out the message that it was med time, I would lollygag along the halls in confused awe at the women running past me and pushing to be first in line.

You would have thought it was a penny candy store the way these women picked and chose which meds they did or didn't want that time. Skip the Tylenol, but make it a double on the Valium. On the opposite end of the line was me. I always stayed as far back in the line as possible. The one night, the doctor prescribed a sleeping pill for me. When the nurse insisted I take it, I refused and pitched a fit. No way was I putting something in my body without researching its side effects and purpose first. Furthermore, they weren't turning me into one of the zombies who had been in the corners of the community lounge area for days. I was relentless in my fight against taking the pill until the head nurse gave in and allowed me to use her computer for fifteen minutes to research the drug on my own. Once I knew it was nonaddictive and lasted no more than six hours, I took it like a good girl. With a half-decent night's sleep, I awoke the next morning with the sun, feeling refreshed.

We got four smoke breaks a day. That was my chance to run and wait for the door to open and for all of us to be buzzed through. As much as I needed the cigarette, I craved the fresh air, even though it was in the nineties with 100 percent humidity out. It didn't take me long to figure out who the moochers of the gang were, bumming smokes with an excuse of a story why they didn't have their own.

There was one patient who arrived on the wing a couple hours after I did. She acted as if she owned the place. Whatever she said, the other girls did. She was the type, if you looked at her funny, she'd make you eat your own teeth. I avoided her not because I was afraid. I simply was turned off by her and didn't like her company. So when she would go out on break I would hang close to the door with the nurse on guard duty rather than go into the courtyard and lounge on one of the wooden benches under the trees. I was watching how she was controlling everyone. If you wanted to sit on any of her benches, she claimed you had to hand over one of your cigarettes. She seemed to have an entourage around her at all times. A few of the clique were reminiscing about the night, on her last stay, when a few of them snuck into her room late at night and she used a paperclip to give them homemade tattoos. Putting two and two together, I discovered that most of these ladies knew one another from previous visits. That bothered me to the same extent as the audacity of this bully.

I asked the nurse standing nearby how often patients return. She replied, "Honey, this place is a revolving door. This may be your first time, but you'll be back a month after you leave."

I flat out told her, "Hell no! Take a picture because you won't be seeing me again. I'm a one-timer."

She responded with hearty laughter and informed me I was a rare one who had just made her day.

Something really funny happened while I was there. It was a sign to me that I was going to get through this. It proved I still had my wits about me and wasn't totally loony. As mentally unstable as I was when I entered, I hadn't lost my marbles completely. It also confirmed another one of my mottoes for life. It's a Jewish proverb that goes like this: "It is better to laugh about your problems than to cry about them."

This is what happened. I was sitting on the side of my bed the first morning after I admitted myself. I was lost in thought, staring down at the medium brown-colored Berber carpeting.

Out of the corner of my eye, I saw something move. I averted my focus to the spot of where the movement was and waited until I noticed it again. I wasn't sure if I was seeing things, so I got down on all fours and just kept watching. I needed personal validation that I was not losing my mind. There were ants crawling on my rug, and there was a small army of them. I went out to the nurses' station and reported it. The young lady on duty called maintenance for me. Lo and behold, it must have been a slow day because maintenance came right up. As I sat in the lounge, I watched the man go into my room, come back out, and stop at the desk before leaving. I later asked the same nurse if they were going to spray, or at least vacuum, my room. She informed me that the maintenance man went in and reported that there were no bugs. Without doubt, the maintenance department was very knowledgeable about these things and couldn't be wrong. I knew what I had seen and didn't appreciate being blown off and assumed to be a nutcase. So, I went back and sat on my bed, watched the ants, and brooded briefly. This nurse and maintenance man were placing a label on me. I needed to remove it before they came at me with the straitjacket.

I had a brilliant idea. A quick look around my room and my eyes landed on my tissue box and my plan was taking off. I finished up in my room and marched, proud as a peacock, to the nurse's desk. I politely asked when maintenance would return. She was kind enough to remind me that the man had come and there were no ants.

I said, "Really? What are these then?" as I showed her the crumpled-up tissue in my hand.

She had the gall to half laugh at me. But she wasn't laughing when I opened the tissue and placed it on her desk. She jumped a mile high out of her seat when she saw the fifteen or so ants that were out of the tissue and scattered on her paperwork. Strike one for the crazy lady. Point made, maintenance not only sprayed my room, they shampooed and vacuumed.

It had been a long while since I could remember laughing. It felt exhilarating. I solved my problem, but did it with humor. It's true that when you find humor in a situation, things won't seem so bad. The laughter does wonder easing the stress. Things could have turned out a lot worse if I had sulked about this and not gotten straight to the point. This was something I kept in the back of my mind throughout my treatment for depression.

I attended each and every therapy session that was on the daily calendar while in the hospital.

I met with a therapist, as well as a psychiatrist, each day. There were three group sessions available to all patients on the wing. Some would take a nap and blow off this part of therapy. But, I was there for me and had no visions of me returning anytime soon. I took advantage of every opportunity to get that piece of advice that was going to bring me back to normal.

I particularly enjoyed the art therapy sessions. Besides making paper flowers out of the entire box of tissues in my room, I was lost without my craft supplies. I needed something to help calm the shaking of my hands. Being in the art room was like heaven to me. I don't think the therapist had ever seen someone so ecstatic about seeing pipe cleaners and glitter before. The therapist quickly realized that arts and crafts were my escape at home and an essential part of me. She so kindly allowed me to keep a ball of sculpting clay to carry around with me. She was my savior at that moment. She and I connected instantly. It dawned on me during one of her sessions that her job would be right up my alley. This would be even better than becoming a teacher. It combined two things that were important to me if I ever had a career: using my creativity and imagination and helping others in need. Another thing that interested about this field was I loved to search for what made others tick. I stayed after our session ended one day to ask her some questions regarding the training needed to obtain a job as an art therapist. It had taken her six years of earning degrees in psychology and art in college. Okay, so maybe it would take me a while to get through college, but it wasn't impossible to achieve. Maybe someday I could start taking courses to work toward those degrees that would be required. The remarkable thing was that I was looking to the future when, only a few days earlier, I had been thinking it was nonexistent for me.

Through group therapy, I realized I was much better off than most of the other patients in the place. In no way do I mean for this to sound conceited. It was the most raw and basic of facts. Of course, others were equally or more depressed than myself. But I didn't have a drug or alcohol addiction added on top of it. I wasn't suicidal. I didn't hear voices telling me to do horrible things to myself or others. I had a home to return to. Some of them lived in the most roach- and rodent-infested places. They had nowhere else to go because that's all they could afford on welfare and had no family to turn to. They had to constantly battle their slumlords for basic necessities like heat, water, and a lock on their front door.

My advantage was having a husband who gave me his full support in every aspect and went out of his way to prove his love for me. I don't recall one of them who had a spouse or even a boyfriend who was looking out for them. Most of them had either been beaten or mentally abused. In some cases, they suffered from both through one or several marriages. The ones who did have husbands had been abandoned with small children and not a dime in their pockets or their other half was serving time in jail for various offenses.

I had stable and wonderful, well-rounded children. I was fortunate to never have to worry where their next meal came from. I heard horror stories from women who had children the same ages as mine. I was grateful that my girls weren't skipping school, doing drugs, shoplifting, or running with older men or a gang. One had a fourteen-year-old who was out prostituting herself. Some were in denial that they had a responsibility to the children. Others had no clue how they had lost control of their children and just gave up and let them run amok. Sadly, others had their children taken away due to lack of parenting or living conditions. Listening to them, I could conclude that their own kids had no respect for their mothers.

I had some issues with my girls, but what came clear to me was they were being normal teenagers. My daughters certainly weren't acting and making decisions as if they were grown adults, and irresponsible adults at best. They were young pre-adults, testing out their adult independence that they knew was just around the corner in the upcoming future. Both of them were honor students and did their best to make my husband and me proud of them. Although the words that came from their mouths at times were out of line, I knew down deep they loved and respected me.

If I didn't realize this before, both my daughters proved it to me during visiting hours and our one family session with the therapist. After the biggest and tightest hugs, their first concern was me and how I was doing. Next was their offer to help me get better no matter what they had to give up. They gave me their heartfelt apologies for any role they played in my being sad and ill. I assured them they were not to blame. It had been a lot of things rolled into one big ball that got me to the hospital. I just needed to unravel that ball and sort some things out. When I tried asking them what they had been up to, they changed the subject back to me. They understood that this was Mommy's time. Shocked at how maturely they were handling this, I looked to my husband to give him credit for practicing with them what to say. He would never lie to me and swore it was all them. He pointed out to me that this is what we had worked so hard for and how we raised them. Just like they knew I would always be there for them, I could say the same that my daughters would always be there for me when I needed them. At that moment, I saw how grown up they both had become and understood I had to let go of them to test out their own wings. I would need to adjust from protective and nurturing mother to one who was there when mentoring and guidance was necessary.

Many of the other patients could see how we interacted as a family during our visits. They were quick to bring it to my attention during group and during conversation at meals and free time. Many of them told me that is what they had wished for with their kids. I felt very lucky—and foolish at the same time for forgetting what I had.

The biggest difference between me and the other patients was I chose to be there rather than being 302'ed by family or court-ordered. Pennsylvania Act 1976 is a law concerning the treatment of acute mentally ill individuals. Section 302 is the part of the Act relating to treatment without consent for observed behavior constituting a clear and present danger to the person and or others. The decision to change the direction of my downward spiral was mine and mine alone. No one else requested that I get help. I denied nothing. Denial played a key role in all these other women's lives. They refused to accept that they were responsible for their current states and situations. But no matter what other characters were in their book of life, they were the stars and had to face the audience and own up to the roles they were playing. Sure, their path would take off in a more positive direction after their stay, some therapy, and the right meds, but they were the only ones to blame if the direction changed again and led them back to the hospital.

I was there for myself first, then my family. It wasn't my family or the court placing me there for my safety and others. By me taking the step and reaching for help, I was prepared for the battle to make changes. Unfortunately, when you are demanded to change, you turn your back on help being provided. Resentment and feelings of betrayal block the view of the positive opportunity placed in your lap. Seeking out firsthand the help to improve allows you to enter a program or treatment with your eyes fully wide open. The willingness to hear and accept your faults and mistakes and to do something about them is a wonderful asset that helps bring forth success from treatment and therapy.

These women couldn't see past their own bitterness to realize that they were showing some type of behavior that caused them to be admitted into the facility. They were so hell-bent against whoever helped have them committed, they failed to see they had serious issues to work on. Nature took over, and they felt trapped, and their main goal was to just get out. So they went through the motions and said what they knew the doctors and therapists needed to hear to gain their release. It was like a big masquerade. Hide the real person so others aren't able to see who's really behind the mask. They would make it as big as needed so they didn't have to recognize themselves. Their recovery from whatever issue they suffered was short-lived. In contrast, asking for my own help, I spoke the truth and faced it. My end results weren't short-term. The mask I wore was temporary and could be lifted permanently. I valued the help I received and made the changes I needed to get control over my depression for a lifetime.

Never did I encounter women like these before. No matter which problem they were being treated for, they closed the door on having a better life. Yet, they had no problem whining and bitching continually about how horrible and wrong their lives were because of someone else. Witnessing them made me appreciate and treasure everything I had been through in life. I was grateful for the gifts I did have. My husband and best friend, my daughters, family, friends, my home, my experiences, my insight, and even my pets were all blessings that I had forgotten about as depression took hold of my body and soul. I had forgotten one of my most treasured mottoes and policies for life. For a while, a number of years back, I was into doing counted cross-stitch. One of the kits I bought and completed from the craft store was of a duck, bear, and dog. Above them was stitched the phrase: *Count Your Blessings, Not Your Problems.* As much as I researched to see who was credited for these wise words, I never could narrow it down to an exact person. There are many similar sayings and old proverbs. I think perhaps this is a very condensed and shortened summary of many of them. Still, the few simple words of common sense make an impact on anybody hearing or reading them.

Even back when I was trying to work through the issues of being molested, I would often sit with pen and paper and just jot down all the good things I had in life. It was a coping tool I used to realize my childhood was horrible, but I still had good things in my life. I stopped doing this, I guess, due to time restraints of daily living. Just like we never forget how to ride a bike, no matter what time span goes by, this was a tool I picked back up on with no delay. The nurses gave me a crayon and some paper, and I had a list a page long before day's end. None of the patients were permitted pens or pencils because these could be used to cause harm and were considered weapons. I would never think of it, but apparently, someone had along the line some-where. Sometimes I would make two columns: one for the good and one for the bad. It didn't matter what the ratio was between the two sides. The good always prevailed over the bad. The good things were the blessings I had received and were priceless and irreplaceable. The bad side consisted of trivial to major issues. Most of them would pass in time or be overcome with effort. For the bad things that appeared per-manent, I had to accept that these were the things I was to learn a life's lesson from. This contradicted why they were in the negative column to begin with. I was going to earn something good out of them eventually. That was another benefit of this simple little coping method. I could see that, even out of bad, good could arise. I urge others who are skep-tical to just try it. It won't cost anything but a few moments of time. Guaranteed, you'll see that the blessings are what count the most. Oh, and feel free to use a pen, pencil, or crayon in the color of your choice.

I not only gained stability in my brief stay in the facility, I regained newfound inner strength, some self-worth, and self-respect before being discharged. I didn't have a clear and defined answer as to why my depression went so deep. Although I had a couple of suspicions, I needed more time to delve into them. I only knew that all my vol-unteer efforts aided and helped bring it to light. Volunteerism didn't cause this it happen. It only emphasized and brought my depression to full light. I had a bunch of goals to aim for, but I needed to take it easy for a little while longer. Before I could narrow down ambitions and dreams, I had to attend outpatient group therapy for six to seven weeks. After that, I would continue on to a therapist for a one-on-one session each week.

Group therapy sessions were beneficial to me. Some patients would tell you that it was a huge waste of their time, boring, and useless. I found the opposite result. A key part of any therapy technique being successful is a desire on the patient's behalf to be part of it. The idea is to help yourself as well as others in this process. In group therapy, another essential key is to be able to listen to others as well as talk. One has to be able to verbally express how they feel. Some find it hard to just open up. That's where an experienced group facilitator comes in handy. He or she has the skills to make a patient comfortable enough to talk. Most of the time, they start by asking simple yes-or-no questions. The more you can talk and let out, the less repressed garbage there will be bottled up inside you.

At the opposite end of the spectrum is listening to the other patients and assisting the therapist. By focusing on what others were saying, I could genuinely hear them. Hearing how other patients were feeling from an experience of their own often copied or resembled something I had felt at one time or at the present. Hearing it vocalized through another's eyes made things click in my brain. Perhaps it was just my intuition working, but I would replay what they had expressed in my mind. I would compare it to myself, process it, and analyze it.

Simply knowing that I was not alone in my feelings and reactions to situations made me feel normal. Hearing another's point of view and combining it with my own allowed me to fully understand many emotions of past and present. Having this reformed view gave me the opportunity to resolve those negative feelings and be that much better off. In the circle, listening to the therapist's and other patients' suggested solutions to problems or the emotions that were bringing me down gave me hope that I wasn't going to be depressed forever. Not every session brought immediate results. But leaving one that initiated a glimmer of hope was well worth my time.

Due to the fact that my outpatient therapy was during the day, there was a conflict between my husband's work schedule and my transportation. For the first two and a half weeks, my husband was still on family leave tending to my needs. All ran smoothly with him there, but he did need to return to work. Because I lived too far outside the vicinity of the clinic, transportation could not be provided. I also did not want to be a burden to family members, begging for rides each day. The only other solution was for me to drive myself there.

On the first morning, I was seriously nervous. My hands were sweating, and every part of me was ice cold, but I managed the first step and got behind the wheel. I stayed the same way all the way to the clinic. The entire drive, I kept repeating out loud that I was doing well. Every mile or at each landmark, I would also vocalize what progress I had made so far. I even managed to park evenly between the lines on the first try once I arrived. Out of the car, I locked up and headed for the sidewalk to the front door. Then it hit me, the adrenalin, the wave of nausea, everything I had held in to get there, and the realization of what I had just done. I barely made it inside the door before my breathing became labored and I collapsed on the floor in a full-blown panic attack. Secretaries leaped over desk to get to me, and a security guard was on the PA system calling some code for a nurse. They got me into a chair, and I just shook and cried uncontrollably until I could get words to come out of my mouth. While the nurse was reassuring me that the worse was over, she gave me a low-dose sedative to help with the jitters. She encouraged me to try again the next day. Her suggestion was to pull over as soon as I felt frightened. If I did that, I might have never left my driveway again.

I tried each day, and each day when I got inside the door to my comfort zone, I would let go of all that I had pent up just to get there and collapse. Each day the attacks were less severe. I only needed the sedative on the first two days. Finally, on day five, I made it all the way past the secretaries, to my therapy room, before finding a chair. I was sitting doing my relaxation breathing when the nurse and therapist walked in together. They were looking at me and asking if I was okay. I looked up at them and nodded my head and let out a joyous "I did it!"

After another week of driving myself, I assured myself that I could do a little more traveling. I found myself stopping on the way home to pick up things for dinner or going a short distance to the pharmacy or produce stand. I felt like a part of me had returned. In time, I was brave enough to make trips not as part of my route to the clinic. I could leave my house and go the complete opposite direction to a department store or the bank. This was a great relief to my husband also. Since I had entered the hospital, all household responsibilities were put on him. He was grateful for the small break and happy to see me coming around. It was a scary time for him, full of worry and upset.

It was at outpatient therapy that I met a young girl no more than eighteen or nineteen years old. I would sit with her and a few of the other patients during lunch and smoke breaks. She was extremely quiet, to the point you could forget she was there sometimes. In one of my first days there, I learned that she had been molested by two male relatives and was trying desperately to cope with it. She had no self-worth and was blaming herself. This sounded so familiar. I would try to offer advice during group when she talked. To be honest, I think I was talking to a wall. She was emotionless, so it was hard to tell if she agreed, disagreed, or even heard me. Rarely was her line of vision ever focused on more than her lap. It pained her to look at someone's face while being spoken to.

The only way I knew she was listening was that she told us one day that she had tried my suggestion of journaling and letter writing. We all told her to write a letter to her molesters telling them how they made her feel. She didn't have to mail it. I even suggested that she address it to herself or her guardian angel, if that helped her start writing. That way there would be no harm if she decided to mail it to herself. The idea was to vent some anger onto the paper. She said she couldn't do it. After a few hours of trying to put the words in her journal, she had page after page of *I hate you* scribbled on them. Many of us took that as a step in the right direction. It was the start of expressing her feelings. Even the therapist patted her on the back for making the attempt, but unfortunately, this poor girl accepted it as another pure failure.

At one of our afternoon group sessions, our therapist drew attention to the fact that we had not heard this girl talk or share for several days. Then she revealed that it did not go unnoticed either that she was wearing long sleeves again and it was the dead of summer. The girl just did not want to answer or look anyone in the eye. She just kept shrugging her shoulders with her hands clasped tightly together in her lap.

Finally, the therapist made her remove her denim jacket. It was obvious to all as stunned silence came upon the room that this disheartened girl had been cutting herself. The sleeves were not because of the cold air-conditioning. They were to hide the deep cuts she inflicted on herself up and down her arms.

Through the questions the therapist was asking, we got the details that had brought her so far down that she needed to cut herself. Obviously, this wasn't the first time she had taken her anger and guilt out on herself physically. The girl's voice was so faint, I struggled to hear her a few seats away. From her account, she had encountered one of her molesters a few days before. He was at her house visiting her family when she arrived home from therapy. She was upset and scared. No one in her family believed that she was telling the truth about what these two trusted individuals did to her. My heart was aching for her. I had to gulp a few times to keep the lump in my throat from growing.

Later that day, she had tried to write in her journal but couldn't put any words on the page. The anxiety pill prescribed by the doctor wasn't helping. She lay on her bed and tried to do some breathing exercises to relax. She became even angrier with herself and needed to calm down. None of the safe methods were working for her. As a result, she went rooting in her drawers for scissors, a razor blade, or anything sharp. Her weapon of choice was a metal nail file found in a manicure kit.

She told the therapist that when she had seen the blood running down her arm, it was like the bad coming out of her. She cut her arms not only to make herself feel better, she did it to punish herself. She told the therapist that she was ugly and deserved what had happened. Although it was faint, she continued talking and next was accusing the therapist of not knowing anything, especially what she had experienced or what she was going through now.

I couldn't contain myself any longer. I stood up and moved a few seats toward her. The tone of my voice was raised due to how much these two relatives pissed me off for destroying her, so she couldn't ignore me. Our therapist at first cautioned me to sit back, but once I started talking to her, she let me take over. I informed this girl that I, too, had the same experiences. She couldn't sit there and tell me that she didn't have the right to live because of being the victim of molestation. It just wasn't going to fly with me.

I did not cease talking, and told her she had the choice to let the men who violated her continue to control her or not. She was not the ugly one. What happened to her was ugly, and so was the cutting. She was very cute, and on the inside she was beautiful. She had to stop wallowing in the darkness and see the light. By not letting the good come forth, she would continue to live in misery. She would just continue to slice her body up until it was ugly and scarred forever. It was her choice to change. These relatives were the evil ones and deserved punishing, not her. If her family denied the truth, that was their problem. Shame was on them. It did not mean she had to shoulder their faults. Most of all, she had to stand up in her own defense for once.

I could tell she could hear me, but had no idea if she was processing any of the words that were coming from my mouth. I just kept talking and making her look at my face. She was crying and nodding her head in agreement with me. I started telling her exactly how she was feeling about herself. She was angry, hurt, unworthy, stupid, ugly, guilty, and wanted to die, along with many other feelings.

Something must have gotten through the thick wall she had put around herself and hit the right spot because out of nowhere she said, "Help me. I want it to stop."

I hugged her tight and told her that was what we were all there for. There was no reason to fear us. And her attackers couldn't hurt her any more than what they already had. I told her that I was living proof that there was a better way of living life and beating the tragedy. I dared her to look directly in my eyes. Still in our embrace, she pulled away and looked at me. A smile came across her face. Suddenly, the whole room was cheering. She was giggling as I turned to see everyone clapping and coming toward us for one massive group hug. No one had ever seen her smile before. It was beautiful, just like what continued, little by little, to shine through from within her in the following days. It was only a muscular movement of the face, but all the other patients knew this was a giant leap of progress for this young girl.

My therapist pulled me from the center of the crowd and gave me my own special hug. She was proud of me and thanked me for helping this girl. I was able to break the ice that she had tried to get through for over three months. I told her there was no need for the individual recognition. I only did the natural thing that a survivor would do for another victim. I couldn't sit back and let her berate and condemn herself, especially when there were two other people who had provoked all her present hardships. It was my duty, in a way, to protect her from them and her own self before any more damage was done. Thinking back over this at home later that evening, the thought entered my mind that perhaps I was a victim all those years ago and our paths were crossing now so that I could be of aid to this dear girl and make a difference in her life.

She wasn't the only one enlightened to the bigger picture through group therapy. As previously noted, I had some ideas how I had become so depressed and needed to work through them. Another patient was telling us how he had become so overwhelmed taking care of his elderly parents and handicapped sister, he forgot to take care of himself. He neglected himself so habitually, he couldn't remember things that he liked and disliked. Essentially, he forgot himself.

Boom! There was the reason for my depression, hitting me like a lead balloon. Now, I knew where the majority of my despair had come from. I didn't know who I was. Always doing for others, I rarely put time into myself. Being a mother determined whether I had the capability to nourish and nurture tiny and young human beings. Parenting shouldn't have defined me as an individual. The same applied in the role as a spouse. Being a wife only proved that I could co-partner the living arrangement we had made together for life. Even as a volunteer for the girls' organization, I wasn't really my own person. I was living the example of what was seen as the ideal adult mentor and volunteer. Take away those three roles, and I could tell you very little about who I really was as an individual. For years, I was hidden in the shadows of others' needs and expectations. I used my roles as a veil to hide behind. Essentially, I masked myself with others' concerns and priorities by taking them on as my own.

My therapy soon switched from daily group to weekly one-on-one sessions with a new therapist. Our goal together was to work on uncovering the mask and finding who I was underneath. For several months, we looked back at my past to see where I had lost my self-identity. We kept searching back further into history until a light-bulb went on. The last time I really knew who I was, I was preparing to confront my brothers. Up until that place in time, I knew myself as a victim. Seemingly after that, I disappeared into other people's needs.

Deciphering where I had taken the detrimental turn gave me the leeway to get back on track. Once I had dealt with my brothers, I had the freedom to be me. Not a victim any longer, I had the chance to be me by my choices, not by the choices or causes someone else had inflicted upon me. Sadly, I didn't seize the moment and run with it. Instead, I meandered around making tons of other people happy. I overcompensated no longer having to hold things back or inside by being open and giving away too much of myself to others. Once all the negative issues of being molested were dissolved, I should have filled the space with finding what really identified me as me. My alternative reaction was to find happiness through other people. I wished for no one to ever be seized by the emotional hardships that I had gone through. The solution I came up with was to give my time and my skills to keep others in harmony and peace. On the same note, I thought that this would be a win-win fix. I thought I could be truly happy by being there for others. Momentarily, it brought me joy and satisfaction to see them grow. But in effect, I wasn't growing. I had stifled myself and made their lives mine. I never put myself at the forefront.

I also wondered why so many years went by from when the depression began and when it brought me to rock bottom. Twelve years elapsed between the meeting with my brothers and my voluntary entrance to the mental facility. Now that I was stable enough and the time was right, I could look back and answer my own question clearly and honestly. For the first ten of those twelve years, I had involved myself with parenting and volunteering. I was content to place myself as second best. Sometime early in the eleventh year, I realized doing for others was not satisfying me anymore. It simply did not do the trick. It finally dawned on me that I wasn't getting a minute in edgewise for myself. I was at an age where I needed to depend on me for me. The time of being dependent upon others to only see a shadow of myself had to end and change.

Recognizing the need and where to start to make things different and become independent from others were two drastically different subjects. My desires and true ambitions had been stagnated by others' needs. Actually, I only knew how to please others, not myself. I had no inkling how to relate to myself and fulfilling my needs.

Thus, the seed of depression had been planted, and it grew and prospered for the next two years. It gradually flourished until I realized the only option I had left was to seek professional and medical help. Otherwise, I would have withered away and died.

If only I had realized this as soon after the meeting with my brothers, I wouldn't have wasted so much time and become depressed. I had basked and floated without a set direction for too long. I repeated once again to myself, *We can't go back and change our past, but we can change our thinking about it.* "If only" were words I had chosen eons ago to not put into use. Easily, one could get caught up in the "ifs" and forget to work on the problem that was supposed to be first at hand. Doing so would result in more delay. Accepting that, for reasons I would never know, I was sidetracked, I chalked it up to a "meant to be" and life-lesson experience that I needed to go through.

I don't consider my long-routed detour a mistake. I don't label anything a failure as long as I keep trying and don't abandon it completely. Surely, it took time passing and a serious bout with depression for me to realize I had forgotten to find me. The fact was I had overlooked myself, but I was now attempting once again to regain myself.

The real work began for me. First lesson learned and drilled into me was saying *no*. This time was about me, not what I could do for others. Initially, when approached with the chance to say it, I stumbled and stuttered to get the simple two-letter word out. Then it became more and more natural to say without hesitation. This had to be one of my first challenges I faced. Otherwise, I could have effortlessly slipped back into being at the beck and call of everyone else but me. After some practice with my new vocabulary word, I was able to pinpoint who simply needed a quick helping hand and who were the life-sucking leeches. You know those type, people who seem to have an entourage of people doing and handing them things. I had to disconnect myself from these types so I could make my life easier rather than theirs.

Appointment after appointment with my therapist, we worked on where I was headed. Although it felt good to vent, the individual sessions didn't seem as effective as group ones. Unlike a group experience, I did most of the talking, and there was little input from the therapist. I didn't feel a great connection with him either. He had the worst habit of patronizing me like a small child. If I told him that I had taken a shower that day, he would pat me on the back and tell me I was being a good girl and helping myself. Still, I kept trying, hoping I'd gain more from the weekly visits.

At about the same time I left outpatient therapy before going one-on-one, I took an acquaintance's offer of attending an astrology class she gave each week in her home. This was something I chose for myself without persuasion or influence from outside parties beyond the initial invitation. The feeling of choosing to do something for myself was invigorating. Learning about the meanings of symbols and numbers on my birth chart was fascinating to me. The odd thing was how precisely it described me and my life. From personality traits, to my spouse, the children I would bear, and special talents, it was all there. The more classes I attended, the more I learned and discovered about myself. I became more accepting of my own faults and took more pride in my positive attributes. Where I could see my faults, I could then work to change or at least improve them. I began to understand relationships I had with other people. Through astrology, I could see what personality types I conflicted or blended well with. I was able to look back on times when I had issues with others and put some things into better perspective. Looking ahead, I could see many possibilities for me.

My teacher and classmates also introduced me to dowsing with a crystal pendulum. From there I started researching different crystals and how their energies would help heal my wounds and soul. Taking great interest in it, I felt it was important to share with my therapist, especially because it was so positive and beneficial to my overall attitude. Certainly, it was motivating me to occupy my mind with something other than depressive thoughts.

He really didn't know much about it. Standoffish, he gave me a "Whatever." He said something along the lines of, "If holding rocks floats your boat, then go ahead."

I was a little put off by his demeanor when he didn't seem to share my enthusiasm or even express an interest to understand the whole idea better. Luckily, I didn't spend too much time causing myself anxiety over this. He was offered a better job and transferred out of that office.

I met with a second therapist for a few months. Success was little with her. Completely opposite, she did have an interest in the metaphysical and holistic, but also had no knowledge. We spent more appointments with me explaining to her how different crystals worked and how to read an astrology chart than we worked on finding solutions for me. In the same way as the first, a better job came about, and she resigned her position. I count this among my blessings. Once again I was putting myself out there for someone else's benefit. The last person I should volunteer for is my therapist. In contrast, she was the last person that should have taken advantage of my willingness. After all, wasn't she supposed to be helping me from falling into that trap again? Things happen for a reason. Unmistakably, it was best that she was not going to be my therapist anymore.

They say the third time is a charm. In my case, it was. I had come to the point that, if sessions with this new one didn't bring success, I was going to give up therapy altogether. When you least expect it, things work out and you get a surprise out of life. My newest therapist was very educated on metaphysical subjects. Added to that, she was well aware of astrology and its teachings. Here it was, almost two years after my stay at the mental facility, and I had finally made that all-important connection with my therapist to fully benefit from my sessions. More than the metaphysical topics, she understood where I was coming from without detailed explanations. Our talks and discussion seemed to flow as if we had known each other for decades. Never once did she snub me for my interest or beliefs. Nor did she ever even hint at abusing my willingness, knowledge or talents. In fact, she encouraged me to use my talents, strive for more knowledge, and to only give myself to others when it was to my full benefit. I found I could trust her with my heart and soul.

She has helped me cope through many struggles. Through hours of discussion, I came to realize that growing spiritually is far more important to me than any career could ever be.

Not that it would be a negative thing to achieve, but it's my top priority that I fully develop myself from within before I go off giving myself to the workforce. Not taking this time, there is great possibility of my relapse back into deep depression. College and a career are still only dreams, but I am okay with that. Through my sessions I have been able to define myself through talents, skills, and qualities I already have. My morals, standards, and what I hold dear in my heart and soul are who I am. I am guided by my intuition and common sense. I have learned not to be embarrassed because I am not book-educated and don't have a very expensive piece of paper to say I know what I read. The street smarts I have, I apply in life daily. These are a testament to the fact that I have honestly lived life rather than having read about it.

Going beyond the mask required me to think from deep within my heart and soul rather than from the emotions I was familiar with on the surface. This just didn't happen at sessions with my therapist. I had to continue this new way of thinking after I left her office, on an every-day basis. Discovering new traits and beliefs, as well as some old ones, allowed me to blossom into my own person. In no means was over-coming the depression and discovering the true me a short campaign. Just about three years after entering the mental facility, I could take all the tidbits and knowledge I had gained and combine them as one big picture. Gradually, as the depression lifted, I began toying with ideas for my future, things I wanted to accomplish and things I wanted to become. Even though my girls were still young, I knew from the bottom of my heart that someday my dream of becoming a grandmother would happen. Easily, I could have set myself up for a relapse. Rather than long-term, unreachable goals, I had to pick and choose ones for myself that were more rational. For instance, I could take a short six-week class at the community center or even the local nature center that offered them rather than going into deep debt registering for full-credit courses.

Faithfully, I took the prescribed medications for depression and anxiety. They were low-dose. Although they seemed to work, I don't believe they would have been as effective if I had been using them alone. To me, drugs lessen or fix the symptoms of depression and anxiety. They are meant to cure the physical aspects of these diagnoses. To fix the cause of the symptoms, one has to use some form of mental medi-cation. This would be seeking out a psychologist or therapist. For some, simply reading self-help books can be the mental remedy that works for them. Others can resolve their mental instabilities with the aid and support of a confidant or friend. All cases are different and require different dosages of mental therapy as well as drugs. Whatever combi-nation it takes is well worth the wait when you find the right one.

Through therapy I flushed out some old habits and developed new ones. One of them was to be more positive. I always did try to find the better side of things, but would get dragged down in the yucky stuff and forget to look to the sunny side of the fence. Another thing that brought me down was other peoples' drama. Equal to the drama were dark and negative personalities of people around me.

I was back to work. My manager, who was naturally the most off-putting person I had ever encountered, made everyone's life miserable. She didn't even have to attempt to be nasty. Her nickname was Darth Vader secretly, because if she knew, she would take it out on the entire workplace, including customers. Her best trait was negativity. Being in her company wore on others sooner or later. Her lousy disposition began to bring me down, and work problems came home with me. She was causing my stress level to rise. Years ago, if I had to be in contact with someone like this woman, I would have backed down and cowered when near her. Not anymore. I chose to fight fire with fire. If she complained, I smiled. If she yelled, I let it go in one ear and out the other. She wanted a response and the attention. I went out of my way to pay her one compliment each day. It irked her to no end. If I commented that her hair looked nice, she'd respond by telling me I had no business looking at her hair. If she threw something like the big metal stapler because it ran out of staples across the room, I'd just duck or go to a different worktable, but certainly did not give her the satisfaction of looking her way. One day, when she threw a fork across the lunch room because it had a particle of food on it from not being washed properly, I was nearby and caught it in midair. Boy, did I piss her off. It didn't bother me that, from that point on, she hated me. I wouldn't want, nor did I need, someone like her on my friends list anyway.

All my coworkers were glum when she was around. Trying to counteract the ill effects, I would share a small joke or extend a compliment their way. As far-fetched as it seems, she eventually had me written up for causing laughter on the work floor. Her claim was that it was a distraction and safety violation. My reaction was to laugh harder, and so was that of the higher bosses. My bosses met with me. They were pleased with my work and attitude and asked that I not let her push me out the door like other employees who had chosen to walk out. Many of my coworkers expressed their concerns to them about her behavior and attitude. Still they kept her on payroll for some unknown, secret reason.

She had serious issues, and I had no intention of making hers mine. One could only imagine what she was hiding behind her mask to make her such a miserable person. The company lost a big account that was more than half our workload. She wasn't the complete reason, but her attitude toward the client didn't help matters and aided in the removal of their business. Rather than having to listen to her about cut hours and the workers standing around waiting for the next job to come in, I requested to be laid off. The timing was perfect. I needed to be away from her. She was one of those dark entities. Evil is a strong word, but she was a good example of what it is. My health was more important than being connected with her. Collecting an unemployment check was okay by me for a little while so I could cleanse myself of any of her aura that may have rubbed off on me. Besides I had a writing project in mind that I could concentrate and put all my energy into. Coincidentally, you are reading it right now.

A few months after I left, a friend who still worked there told me it only got worse. Staff for our department went from twelve people to three. One by one they got up in the middle of a job and walked out because she cast a straw that broke their camel's back. Shorthanded and with a big job coming in the front door, the head boss told this manager to call me in to work. She refused and threw a temper tantrum. The bosses were finally growing tired of her antics, as well as her disrespect for people. She was sent home for the day without pay. No offense was taken on my part. As a matter of fact, I laughed for days about it. The quality time I was spending at home wasn't up for bargaining, not even to be exposed to her bitterness for just one day. I could feel and see the difference in me not having someone with her qualities invading my personal zone. So, I distanced myself from her and those like her to keep my life drama- and stress-free.

Each and every person who is in my life plays an important role where my mental state is concerned. Those who are pessimistic, demanding of me to be different or change, are not beneficial to me. It takes constant effort to keep your mood up once you've suffered from real depression. Much of the energy you have inside goes toward keeping up your self-esteem, self-worth, and self-respect. Allowing myself to be surrounded by people who express negativity or make me feel inferior, I run the risk of all the above to be lowered.

If not careful, these vital ingredients of stability can be lessened to the point of loss. The end result would be another bout of depression that could take just as much, possibly more time, to bounce back from. To be honest and fair, I could not blame anyone else for the relapse but myself. I gained the knowledge through therapy what happens to me by associating with a certain type of people. I am very sensitive to my surroundings, and people as well. Choosing to interact with these wrong types is equivalent to saying I want to risk my stability.

Naturally, I'm going to encounter these kinds of people throughout life. I cannot quit jobs or lock myself in my house each time one crosses my path. This is where my judgment of others' character comes into play. At first sight that a person could be detrimental to my positive outlook of my own self, I've trained myself to create that necessary distance as soon as possible. Pursuing further connection with one of these individuals makes the breakaway even harder. If it is a situation such as work, I remain civil and respectful, but in no way allow that person to get any closer to me. They say there is one of those negative or nasty types at every place you ever work. There's no doubt in my mind that there is. I just know better than to feed their ego or feed into their drama. In my heart, I believe my former manager at the printing company was one of the worst I will ever encounter. Luckily, time was working on my behalf; I seized the opportunity, requested the layoff, and got out of her poisoned air.

Another thing I learned through therapy was to stop procrastinating and to prioritize my daily chores and long-term goals. I used to find myself putting off tasks because I was feeling down, and that drained my physical energy. The more I put something off, the more down I'd get and fault myself even more. Prioritizing was important to keep things balanced and to deter being overwhelmed.

In one of my sessions, I completed worksheets where I had to list my goals for the day, the month, a year, then five years, and ten years. Prioritizing at the end of each list caused me to think logically and rationally about the period I chose for each task. I found myself moving things around to more appropriate time spans. Above all, I realized I do not have Superwoman's power. When I make my list now, I note what is absolute necessary to get done by marking those items with a star. If I tackle more than these things, I count them as a blessing.

Big dreams were put aside to wait for brainstorming when the time is right. Having been so focused on long term goals and reaching them,

I forgot about what was important at the current moment. Complete remission of depression was foremost and aimed at for every waking minute. For this to be possible, I had to learn to take one day at a time. Rome wasn't built in a day and neither will my ideal world.

My ideal of being a good mother, wife, daughter, spouse, and so on was holding me back from being myself. In turn, I felt insignificant and a failure. Truth be told, my opinion changed drastically through therapy. Naturally, I was skeptical at first. But if I wanted my life to change, I had to be open to looking at it from different angles. It's not the material things I possess or have earned that make me a person. Completely assured now, I believe that family, friends, and acquaintances are signs of what I have already achieved. Having these assets proves, no matter what else I am or become, I still hold the greatest rewards. For they are who have cheered me on in my setback, and they will be beside me with each victory I claim. The material things connected to me will never give me a thumbs-up or a big old pat on the back. Where and what I do for a paycheck should not be a primary concern, provided that I am helping make ends meet when it comes time to pay bills. Never will a paycheck or my job status compare or hold precedence to the pureness of coming into my home and seeing my family or sipping on a cup of tea with a good friend close by. I can always find or replace a job. I cannot replace a loved one if I were to lose one of them. Habitually, I take time to stop and just look at the special people interacting in my life. Taking photos of them and the things we share is a new habit as well. It is important to reflect on my treasure and memories often.

Just as I have learned that things happen in a precise manner at the time that is appropriate, I've equally learned God does not give you more than you can handle. Of course, while situations are occurring, it seems he is over-testing us, pushing the limits to the brink of begging for mercy. Looking back at different episodes of my life, especially the molestation and depression, I understand God knew I was strong enough to get through it and come out a better person. It was I who didn't know my own strength and capabilities. Through all my experiences, whether they were good or bad, I learned to have faith and trust myself more. One may believe God wants us to plead for mercy and suffer. In reality, he doesn't wish that for us. It pains him to watch us go through struggles as much as we hate the experiences. He, be-

ing the Almighty and the all-knowing, understands we need those obstacles to grow, just like the butterfly that can't be given the easy route.
Guaranteed, though, he is our greatest cheerleader at every step we take
to overcome and expand.

CHAPTER 11

Step 12 or Something Like That

By now I had turned myself inside out and knew myself from every angle. Severe depression was no longer a major worry. I had gained tremendous self-confidence compared to the former me. I was living life by my rules, values, and choices that had I decided upon. I had the strength to stand by my opinions and defend my beliefs. While I still listened to advice thrown at me, I decided on my own what to do with it. My head was clear of negative self-talk and damaging feelings. It would be a lie to say all my days were sunny and full of rainbows. Down moments and days still existed, but not on a regular basis as they had in the past. I had the ability, with an array of coping skills, to combat against them.

Finding time to keep in touch with my individuality was a key part of leading a stable and normal life. A short meditation each day helped to keep my mind focused. Meditation is not only a relaxation technique. It provided me with the opportunity to keep a connection between the physical parts of me and my heart and soul.

During one of my regularly scheduled visits with my therapist just over a year ago, I asked to discuss something I had been tossing around in my head for a few months. There really was no need to ask. We always talked about whatever topic I felt I needed to bounce about or vent completely on.

I stated that I was sure that I had missed something in my recovery from being molested. My therapist simply asked, as a concerned friend would, why I felt this way after being free for so long. That's what I could count on from her. She never once gave me the deer-caught-in-headlights stare when we discussed the path I had taken to get beyond the paralyzing experience and effects. She had always justified to me how I deserved a great deal of credit for going about the healing process mostly by intuition and faith.

With ease I answered her question. I took a few minutes to explain where my thinking had come from and where it brought me to. It came about one day while sitting on my patio daydreaming. My mind wandered back to all I had had to do to get over the pain of molestation. I was proud of my accomplishments. I have to confess that I am my own worst critic. I began to think how I would have done things differently. Little came to mind. Deep in my heart, I knew each fear and heartache was necessary for me to reach the end. A shorter amount of time in getting there was the only thing that waddled to the surface of my brain.

There went my mind onto another trail. How could the vast frame of time have been reduced? Perhaps I should have sought out professional help. Perhaps having someone to talk to and get advice from would have sped things up. Then again, I recalled the many sagas of people who had spent decades in treatment and therapy and had made minimal progress. The idea of how my rehabilitation time could have been shortened was not the missing piece of my recovery. Then I went blank, before questioning what methods or resources existed that I could use. Like the cheese standing alone, one came to mind. I doubted Alcoholics Anonymous was the program I needed. Still, it was the only prospect I had to mull over at the time.

I started thinking about what knowledge I did have about AA. Sorry to say, the list was vague and contained the bare minimum of information. I was aware that meetings were held several times a day in a wide range of locations in a great percentage of communities throughout our country. Meetings were a place for alcoholics to receive and share support with their addiction. Similar to group therapy, coping skills, situations, and challenges people are struggling with are all discussed. On the trivia side of things, the girls at the mental facility had told me they say the Serenity Prayer, written by Reinhold Niebuhr, at the start of each meeting. Because of them, I recite this same prayer when I am struggling with my own obstacles. While I am saying it on my behalf, I cannot help but think of those girls and pray that they are well and living by the words still.

Through word of mouth and media of various types, I had always heard AA linked with the term "Twelve-Step Program." I didn't know what each step entailed. I only gathered that you couldn't make it to number three by just jumping over the first two. I went out on a limb and assumed some of the steps were similar to the steps I had gone through in my recovery: I had to admit that the actual molesting and aftereffects were a serious problem in my life. I had to accept my responsibility for allowing this to be the way I would go through life, or I could make the decision to fight to bring forth the good. I had made my amends with my brothers. Then there was the last one I always heard mentioned often, giving back and sharing.

There it was. That is what I had missed out on. I did not go out and share my experience with other victims. Finding a way to help other molestation victims find peace with their past trauma is what I should have aimed at doing once I had my freedom from it. I was never more confident in my life of what I needed to do. It was what I decided I needed to tackle in my newfound security of being me.

I thought back to the young girl I had met in the outpatient clinic. I did help her. But a few days after she seemed to have her first break-through, I was released and referred to the one-on-one therapist. I had no way of knowing what her outcome was. I prayed that she had continued to heal and found happiness in her life. As for me completing this last and final step, I needed the validation that my anguish and triumphs could inspire a positive difference in another victim's life. Not out of selfishness, but because I truly believed God did not place this challenge before me and see me through for my individual gain. I was meant to be his assistant, in a way, and share my good news so someone else could also benefit from my reward. To go a little deeper, if it were his only son who had gained from an experience such as I had, he would without doubt go to the nearest mountaintop and share what he had learned along the way to triumph. After all, to live in the image and likeness of his son and to love one another is about all God expects of any of us.

Turning back to my therapist, who said little while I talked, she was nodding her head in agreement. Now I had to decide how to go about it, and this was where I needed her suggestions and encouragement. Without hesitation, she told me to write. It made perfect sense to me. Expressing my feelings on paper had always come more naturally to me than verbalizing them. I had always been writing lists and on occasion jotted out poetry here and there. Journaling was one of my newer habits also. I don't understand why I didn't see the obvious at the start. In the end, it was the most practical and logical choice for me to follow through on.

Her advice to me was to keep it on the smaller side. Maybe I could find a nonprofit victim support group to submit an article to. She suggested definitely not to write so much that I had enough pages to turn into a made-for-TV miniseries. Article size was going to be a challenge because when a pen hits my hands and I start writing, the thoughts just flow uncontrollably at times. A TV movie seemed like a never-ending story and a tad unreachable. Besides, that option would require so much dedication, I ran the risk of resenting it, becoming bored with it, and tossing it in the wastebasket incomplete. Somewhere in the middle would satisfy my needs and place my goal in foreseeable reach.

I think I skipped out the door that evening as I left her office. I had never felt so secure and determined about an idea before. This was a project about me, for me, and I held all control. It was brought about by no other influence than my own soul-searching. Actually, I have to include the support of my therapist on that.

I wanted this bad enough that I made the time. In a peculiar way, I desired this more than overcoming my childhood. Never had a creative endeavor been so important to me. Very easily, I could get distracted and consumed with a minute household task. As they say, a mother's work is never done. I had to really focus on what was priority and what could be set aside to free up the time to dedicate to this project. As much as I wanted to just close up shop and bunker down with pen, paper, computer, and my thoughts, I needed to clear the way. There were some issues within my home that were just near complete. My husband and I had become foster parents the previous fall. We took in a family of three siblings. Each one of them had their own individual mental and physical problems that needed to be dealt with. It was an overwhelming experience, and my workload tripled. Somehow I managed to find some free time every so often to escape the monotony. It was never quite enough time to sit down and focus on writing, though. Determined to keep my plan within reach of reality, I would at least jot down memories or ideas of what I wanted to convey in my writing. Scribbling out a rough paragraph about once a week was about the extent of what I could accomplish to keep my project in the line of vision for me.

The long-awaited news arrived in late spring. Two of the children would return home shortly after the school year ended. The third would be transferred to a group home setting. We celebrated with them. Equally, we rejoiced for ourselves and a job well done. It had been a tough situation, but I was anxiously ready to take on my new adventure of writing.

It took me several attempts to find what my first words would be. As a warm-up, I practiced with a short one-to-two page summary and writing an article. I had so much to express. I was finding it impossible to narrow it down to a few paragraphs. Perhaps later on, once I've gotten it all out, I can pinpoint one aspect of my experience to shed light upon with its own feature story.

I did have my hesitations about writing a very personal story such as mine. In the back of my mind, I had a slight fear that recalling all the memories and feelings would pull me back into the darkness. Rehashing old feelings can be bad news. Throughout the time it took me to write my story, I surprised myself and never once had a negative feeling return. The pursuit of vocalizing the past into visual words was, in a way, a chance for me to test my self-trust. The challenge would be to see what I would do if the negative feelings of anger and resentment returned. By writing it all out, I had the feeling of relief, satisfaction, and fulfillment. This further proved to me personally that I am fully recovered. I am a survivor.

When I type the last word on the last page, I do not know where the entire collection of pages will end up. There are plenty of directions they could go. At the moment, I am unsure what avenue to proceed on. What I can say as fact is that, even though putting all this into words proved more rewarding for me than I expected, my main intention is to reach out to help others who have suffered like I did.

I can look back and openly view how much worse my entire life could have been. If not for the phenomenal support of my husband and me opting for the good over the evil path, I could have been lost forever. To think that there are victims out there with no one to reach out to, I get chills up my spine. To know there are victims out there who just cannot get a grip strong enough to reach out or take help when it is offered is very saddening. To understand that there are probably victims of molestation who had their self-esteem ripped from them would cut, harm themselves, or end their life tragically, without anyone knowing their secret and how they have suffered, is sickening. If there's a remote chance I hold the key for the sufferer of one of these situations, I have to attempt to open the door for them, even if it's only a crack.

I have survived a volatile mistreatment at the hands of not one, but three molesters, and to not reach out to tell another victim that I care that they are hurting would be shameful and selfish on my part. I am far from that type of person. I believe it is my duty and my destiny to help someone become a survivor. It is not only meant to be the final step of my childhood journey. My challenges and defeating them are meant to be the beginning for another victim.

In Chapter Five, I wrote that I was not exactly sure where my insight came from. It either came with me at birth or I developed it. No matter how it ended up with me, it is a blessing from God above. When I get those hunches to act or not act on something, I believe they are miraculously put in my mind by a guardian angel or spirit guide that he has sent to guide and protect me. I feel I owe him the graciousness for these special gifts he has given to me by reaching out to his other children who are suffering in the same way I did. I cannot think of a better way to repay him than by sharing my insights with others so that they may heal and grow spiritually too.

I have been rewarded throughout life many times over. My children and husband, along with the rest of my extended family, are those I hold dearest. I pray often for the continued guidance and strength I need to cope so I may continue to grow. But the reward I pray to be granted one day is to hear another victim say, "Thank you for sharing your gifts and your life. You helped change things for me."

And as I near completion of my final pages, that is the only outcome I wish to see from the efforts I place here. If I do not get to help someone through these pages, then I will not consider myself failing. For someday, at another time, the person or persons I know in my heart who I am destined to help will cross my path.

CHAPTER 12

Today, It's Amazing

When I became aware of the necessity to cease thinking and pressuring myself about the future, I had to guide and force myself to live in the moment. I had to slow my pace by several miles per hour. Once I started taking a few minutes here and there to relax and clear my mind from the rat race of daily routine, I realized, sitting quietly alone with my thoughts, I had missed out on many awe-inspiring moments. This dealt with only me and Mother Nature, so to speak.

I had noticed something back in the mental facility. More than getting out for the cigarettes, I went out just to have the sun beat on my skin. Not in the aspect of sunbathing, but sitting and really connecting with the ball of fire in the sky. Never before had I really paid attention to the feeling of how the sun's rays spread and smoothed across my face. The warm, energizing touch on my arms and legs was comforting. It seemed to be unconditionally sharing its own strength and powers with me in a soothing and peaceful manner. It was almost as if the sun was injecting some sort of positive vibes into me from the skin inward. It made me feel strong and motivated. For those short three days in treatment, I craved sunlight. I wanted that natural massage and therapeutic feeling. We had lots of light inside, but none of it natural. Being in the strong fluorescent lighting for so many hours a day gave me a tremendous headache and I swear made me edgy. The whole wing gave me bad vibes. So here I was Little Miss Homebody, antsy to get outdoors.

Never could I imagine missing the place. But I missed those few moments each day being out and exposed to fresh air and real lighting.

Added to my daily routine, it is now mandatory that I sit outside at least ten to fifteen minutes. Catching the breeze from the bench on my front patio is the norm. I try as often as I can to find time to head to a state park nearby. A walk on the trail to the Delaware River or a stroll through the woods always leaves me feeling revitalized, especially when under a lot of stress. It is not just the sunlight that I crave anymore. I enjoy nature. It is so breathtaking. I now treasure the simple moments, like when I come upon a patch of buttercups in a field, standing brightly all alone, or seeing a hawk take off from a tree and soar in circles above so gracefully. When I can remember, I take a camera along with me to grab a shot when these sparkles of surprise pop up. Looking back at the nature photos I've taken reminds me of the good feelings I got the second my eyes spotted the subject.

My most favorite nature escape is time spent at the beach along the Jersey Shore. I'll take any beach or ocean as a view. I'm not picky. The sound of ocean waves and the breeze, along with the sun shining down on me, is the most soothing feeling I have ever felt in my entire life. I've been going to the shore since I was a teenager. I never noticed its natural beauty until after my bout with depression. I now fully appreciate it being there. I rely on its constant and stable pattern to be there when I need a spiritual and mental cleansing. When I go to Cape May, I have an added benefit to treasure. I make it a point to route down Jackson Street to a small metaphysical shop I discovered a few years back. The wave of positive energy that rolls through me upon entering the door of The Guardian and taking a few steps inside is as uplifting as the ocean. It must come from the energy of all the crystals and positive items stocked on the shelves. No trip to the shore would be complete without a stop by the store. What a blessing it is to have a double dose of positive therapy in a short amount of time. The added benefit of gaining the friendship of the owners is also another of my many blessings.

During group and individual sessions, it is always stressed and drilled that exercise is mandatory. Well I am not going to say the professionals are wrong. Let me just say I also can never imagine me receiving an Exercise Buff of the Year award. I can agree with the idea that moving about, using your muscles, does help with battling depression. To be up and have the juices flowing is much better than sitting in a chair, unmotivated and sullen. This can be said whether depression exists or not.

There are more than physical benefits of exercise. The psychological and mental benefits can improve the symptoms of depression and anxiety as well. Yes, exercise can improve our physical appearance. Seeing the improvement makes us feel better about ourselves, thereby increasing our self-confidence, self-worth, and self-acceptance. Being physically active, whether through an exercise program or simply walking around the neighborhood, leaves one with a sense of accomplishment.

Sitting and dwelling on how bad you feel is not good at all. Being so focused on the negative intrudes on resolving the actual issue and coping with it in a healthy manner. I know the more I sat and wallowed in self-pity, the more depressed I became. Getting up and exercising takes the focus from the damaging thoughts to more pleasant ones. If you can't motivate yourself to exercise, you should at least attempt another form of physical activity, like bowling or washing your car. Heck, there are days I clean out closets for hours just for the sake of movement, rather than sitting, sulking, and accomplishing nothing.

On the comical side of things, I did listen to peoples' advice that yoga was a great way to get exercise, as well as free your mind. It made sense. I could sit and meditate, and I could also exercise. Why not try yoga? It seemed to be merely a combination of the two. All gung-ho, I purchased a beginner's DVD and set up in my living room in front of the TV. In the first few minutes, it was proven that I am no longer the young teenager who could lift and put both my legs behind my head and rock on my butt. I tried following the DVD a few more times, thinking I'd improve. Just like some people cannot chew gum and walk at the same time, I couldn't get down the right breathing rhythm and stretching at the same time. I was like a bull in a china shop, clumsy and awkward. My family got a good laugh watching me try to keep up. I'd be rolling off my mat when I was simply supposed to sit in a relaxed Indian-style position. I'll admit to it, I am a klutz and have the coordination of a turtle. As much as I wanted yoga to be for me, we didn't find the connection that millions of others have.

When I was depressed, I had the overwhelming feelings of being alone and isolated from all other people. Exercise gives the opportunity of socializing and interacting with others. Places like gyms, parks, and your neighborhood are all places to exercise. Equally, they are places where you can meet people. When I take a walk around my neighborhood, I don't go with the intention of meeting or socializing. By chance, some days I run into a neighbor and end up stopping to have a quick conversation before going back along my way. At times, I'll just pass someone and exchange a smile or friendly hello. Those are the days I'm really glad I went because the feeling of loneliness that strikes at times is lifted and I am in a much better frame of mind when I return home.

There's no need to deny it, I still have my share of low days every now and again. They are nowhere near as often as they used to be. In the worst case now, the longest length of depression is no more than a few days before I am back up. I expect these days, and I accept them. Life would be pretty boring if it were always filled with roses and rainbows. Sure, I'll take roses any day of the week. But thinking logically, all roses come with thorns. So if I want the roses, I have to take the thorns with them. Easily, a down day can turn into a long-term depression by me becoming angry over it or taking it as a fault against myself. I still have moments where I unnecessarily beat myself up on occasion. When the bad days do come about now, I go along with the flow and just do what I have to do. I apply my coping skills so that it will pass much more quickly than if I ponder on it and make a big to-do about it. Low days are like dogs begging for a bone. If you don't give them the attention they want, they'll go away and lie back down.

It's nearing the sixth anniversary of my breakdown. Knock on wood, I have not had a day where I felt as pitiful, hopeless, and helpless as I did on that fated day. I have total faith in myself to never sink that low ever again.

There is no doubt in my mind that the day I signed myself into the facility was the worst I had ever had in all my life. Totally in opposition, I know it was one of the best days I will ever have in this life. God forbid, if I had given up and come to the point of considering taking my life, I plainly would not be here now. Any growth that I had potential for would have dissolved along with me. Putting myself there, in professional hands, allowed me to continue. It was the start of a whole new life, or at least a new outlook, and it added more value to my existing one, which was about to change dramatically.

Each year on the anniversary of this personal and historical day, I celebrate. It is now the date each year that I call my re-birthday. I spend the day putting attention on me. It's a day of reflection, where I look upon where I was and how far I have come. This is the day I renew the promises I made to myself: I would live life as me, not by another's standards or needs. I would never be that destructive to myself ever again. I cherish the good things and times in my life and look for the blessing or lesson to be gained in the hard times.

To keep these promises, I have to be tuned in and aware of what exactly is causing me to feel a certain way at a given moment. Also, "no" is still frequent in my vocabulary. I remain alert to changes in my mood.

There are an abundant amount of things that can sway my mood. What I have to be guarded against are those things that can create a mood that can lead into depression if unchecked. People, the weather, stress, and boredom can all be the trigger that brings me down. Added to the list would be my own ability to talk down to my own self. In order to stay true to myself and my promise, I can't let these things slide. I have to face them immediately and counteract.

When it is a person or a group causing me the negative feelings, I usually enforce one of two solutions. I let them know exactly how they are making me feel or what it is they are doing that is the problem. The other tactic is to remove myself from their presence. The severity of the situation accounts for how long the time span is regarding further interaction with them.

Depending on the case, I decide on which of these solutions I act upon. Sometimes it's just the first, if that is all that is needed. Then again, there have been times when I proceeded to the second option without the first. It's not mandatory I go to every argument I'm invited to. Yet other times, I have needed to apply both tactics when necessary.

There's also the old rule when dealing with difficult people: kill them with kindness. It could be a coworker, the girl at the checkout counter in the grocery store, or someone you live with. It doesn't matter who, what, or where the person is. When someone is ejecting there negative attitude or feelings into the air, just put the equal amount or more of a positive attitude up there against it. Most of the time, it either ticks off the difficult person and they go away on their own or it baffles them as to why you aren't following their suit. Combating their negative with a tiny compliment may be all that is needed to change their whole mood to a better one.

When being brought down by the weather, stress, or boredom, I resort to my wide array of options for prevention. One of my biggest downers is the weather. On rainy, gloomy days, I keep occupied with cleaning or reading. Other times, I may sit and go through my photos from trips to the beach or other sunny and cheery pictures I've taken. Drawing or painting with bright, vibrant colors is another pick-me-up. The winter months, when there may not be as much sunlight for me to bask in, are harder for me.

When it is stress or anxiety interfering with my harmony, I rely on my coping skills. Relieving the effects of the two is as important as resolving the cause. Doing both is essential to prevent being brought down further. Heading into a hot, noise-free bath can do the trick sometimes. Throw in some of my favorite scented candles, and it is pretty much a guarantee I'll be less tense afterward and more capable of handling the load.

I now own a wide variety of relaxation CD's. My collection consists of various nature sounds, guided visual meditations, soft musical melodies, Celtic instrumentals, and vocal music. I've purchased them from metaphysical shops, bookstores, and flea markets. Popping one into my player and escaping for thirty minutes helps me face the stress when I return.

At other stressful times, I may grab my dog and her leash or and take a stroll around the block. That few minutes away may be all I need to make the problem I have to finish dealing with less straining.

There is an option that is always available to me if I am really struggling with relieving the stress. My psychiatrist gave me a prescription to calm my nerves and reduce my anxiety level. When I was in the facility, and for approximately a year after, I took the medication on a daily basis. Although it is a very mild dose, I would rather work through issues on my own. It is not because I am afraid of dependency or side effects. It is a personal choice to rely on myself before seeking it out. I also want to know that it is there and will work for me when I turn to it. Taking it on a regular basis could cause my body to build up a tolerance, causing it to not be effective when I may need it the most. I completely understand that other people suffering from panic and anxiety disorders must take relaxants on a daily basis as I did in the past. It is to be admired that they are doing what they need to do to cope and get through their ordeals. My case is no longer as severe as what it was a few years back. If I run to the bottle and swallow a pill at every sign of stress, I'd be denying myself the chance to apply the coping skills I have acquired. My thinking is that all the work I have done learning to face and work through problems would be useless. I prefer to apply a tool that comes from within me than one that is put in me chemically. The medication does what it is supposed to when I do take it. It does take that edge off my nerves so I can focus on what I need to be doing. Although their frequency is rare, taking a pill when I feel a panic attack coming on halts them before progressing any further. Still, just the fact alone, knowing that the medication is there for me is, comforting enough to ease some of the pressure on me at times.

What tool I use with stress and anxiety also depends on what type of situation is causing the stress to rear its ugly head. Two years ago, my youngest daughter was the passenger in a friend's car when this fairly new driver's poor judgment caused a very serious accident. Thank God, the girls all walked away, because it could have been fatal. My daughter was the only one with injuries. Her knee was crushed. She suffered excruciating pain and had to use a wheelchair. A month afterward, she had surgery to put screws in for support.

Without it, she would suffer other problems later down the road. There were many days of crying, anger, and sheer frustration. My place was to be nowhere but by her side. Suddenly she went from a very active and social teenager to a helpless invalid. I helped her dress, shower, and get from room to room. When she was hospitalized, all I could do was sit by her bed and get her whatever she needed. I understood perfectly that this was not me-time, but there were times that I needed a break from the stress of it. I couldn't leave her, so I couldn't apply many of the coping skills I normally turn to. In between taking her to the bathroom and the many other things she was dependant on me for, I tried to write in my journal. It was hard to do with frequent interruption. My entries during that time are a little garbled and short.

The one thing I could do as I sat by her bed or while assisting her with her needs was to pray.

Praying is one of the few tools that can be done while multitasking. No one knows you are doing it. For sure, you don't need special equipment like a pen, electrical outlet, or your voice to do it either. All you need is your thoughts, your intentions, and someone to hear you. I asked that she have a full and the speediest recovery possible. I called upon my higher powers to give her the strength and determination to get through this. Because this accident could have had a much worse outcome, I knew instantly that it was a meant-to-be experience. I truly believe it was a karmic event. I pleaded that for all involved to have the insight to see the blessing they received that day and accept the lessons we were all supposed to learn from this. Praying gave me the strength needed to get through the worst days in the first few months. After I've put my hopes and wishes out there to a power higher than myself, I'm left with more hope that they will be heard and granted. Letting go and handing them over gives me the courage and self-confidence to keep pushing through the challenges.

In my daughter's case, she has learned a great deal about "friends" versus true friends during her healing time. She realizes that things could have come out differently that morning. For such a young age, she knows how quickly things can change and be taken away. She is grateful for every step of progress she makes in recovery. She had much time while recuperating to reflect and learn to count her blessings also. With the surgery and physical therapy, she is walking again. At home, she can get around on her own now. Getting around school was an issue at first. She still used a wheelchair because she hadn't mastered steps, ramps, and hills. By continuing the physical therapy, prayers, and thinking positively, she accomplished them all.

When it comes to boredom, there is no excuse to sit and sulk. In the event that I do not go find something to overcome it, I sit and brood. I nitpick at myself. I find fault in myself and the things I have and what I have accomplished. It's a terrible trait to allow yourself negative self-talk. It just sets you up for defeat. It can collapse all the good that is built up in you.

There is a fine line between habit and addiction. I discovered back when I was in the mental facility that negative self-talk was something I did to cause my own dilemma. It took me a while longer to realize it had crossed over from nasty habit to compulsive addiction. I had to work long and vigilantly to stop the obsession of it. It was hard at first. I had to learn to listen to myself. Each time I caught myself, I had to follow it up with a positive reinforcement. Eventually, I'd catch myself before I got the thought completely finished and quickly insert a positive attribute about myself.

Well aware of my triggers, I know boredom can lead to this self-abuse. At first hint that I need something to do, I don't sit for long. I turn to my resources. Crafting, sewing, gardening, surfing the Net, and grooming my dogs are among my library of choices. If I can't find interest in any of these and more, there is at least a pen and pencil around to doodle with. It's really hard to be depressed while doodling silly faces or exaggerated, goofy-looking flowers.

Other times I may sit with my cases of crystals and do some meditation. I have different crystals for different purposes. Some may be for bringing me things like calm, cheerfulness, insight, memory enhancement or clarity. Yet, others bring forth physical things such as pain relief or restful sleep. Meditation brings me many of these same results. After completing a meditation, I am more focused, relaxed, and levelheaded. Combining the two tools by holding or placing some crystals around me while meditating, enhances the mediation and the benefits from it. Together or separate, these are coping methods that help me achieve the positive aspect I am looking for and removes negativity.

I have always been drawn to this particular art form I'd see now and again. I didn't know the name until doing a search on the Internet. The art I had been seeing for eons is known as mandalas. Normally the pictures or paintings are circular in shape with an object or symbol in the center. All around the center are layers of circles in consecutively larger sizes. Each circle or ring would flow into the next. The inside of each would also be filled with patterns, similar to that of stained glass. Many are done in vibrant, eye-catching colors. I always got a spiritual feeling or one of inspiration when looking at one. On the Internet, I found sites that allow you to print out plain ones to color on your own. There are also many workbooks available to purchase online and at bookstores.

Coloring in one of the blank mandalas, even for just a few minutes, aids my body and mind. There are no rules or expectations regarding how I choose to fill in the spaces or how I interpret them. Pulling out my pencils and blank sheets creates a positive energy to be formed around me. When sitting and working on mandalas, it allows me to create a calm and peaceful environment around me. There could be total chaos happening in another room, but for the moment, it's just the crayons, paper, and me.

When first looking at mandalas, they can seem to be big blotches of circles and lines. Giving them the second glance they deserve, the orderliness of the design can be seen. There are definite patterns visible. Coloring in the patterns helps create order in me. I can regain perspective on what I need to be focused on and place things where they belong. The symmetrical repetition of the patterns and shapes naturally draws the eye to the center, bringing forth focus.

Others would say that mandalas are a visual path of the universe with the core being God. I have not gotten that deep or been able to think of them in those terms. After coloring loads of them, I use them to relate to myself. I see myself and my energy in the center. The outer circles are what I give off or put forth. As they graduate in size toward the largest outer edge, I relate them to the cause and effect I have on others, situations, and things. The furthest outer circle from the center would represent the final outcome or what I need to work and aim for.

From the opposite direction, I see the outer circles as things I need to gain, learn, improve, remove, or change. As the circles lead inward to the core, where I am, I can relate how the outer circles impact me and become part of me.

Not always does it have a soul-revealing effect. But when it does, I listen to it. Sometimes, it's just creating that space and working with the colors that I benefit from. No matter what result I get, I have provided myself with the time to relax, practice some self-therapy, and gain serenity. The act of coloring, whether it is mandalas or little-kid coloring pages, leaves me with wonderful therapeutic effects in place of boredom and stress.

When my mood is affected negatively in any way, I, on occasion, have the tendency to bake.

Placing my focus on a recipe so that I follow it accordingly doesn't allow room for anything else, especially stress or other negative emotions. Baking one treat usually suffices.

I have been known to go on baking marathons. The end result is a choice of two to three things for my family to snack on. When at my worst stress levels, I bake until nearly every ingredient I have on hand in my pantry is used up. If I run out of things to bake, I turn to cooking. I keep going until I've burned off all the stress and negativity that was eating at me. It's always been a habit to clean as I go along with the baking process. When I am done, I am left with a clean kitchen, and my home is filled with the wonderful scents of a grandma's house and a display of homemade baked goods on my table.

One time when I was under major stress and it was causing me to deal with insomnia, I went on the largest marathon my family has ever witnessed. They awoke in the morning to find I had made coffee cake, brownies, pudding, chocolate chip cookies, and apple and pumpkin pies. That was bad enough, but to their shock, I added baked ziti, chicken casserole, meatballs, sausage, potato salad, a small turkey, and a pot of soup. They thought I was completely off my rocker. But no, I was feeling wonderfully rejuvenated. Sure, I was tired, but I was no longer worried or feeling the weight of stress. As I baked, cooked, and cleaned, I worked through the problems causing me the hardships and realized there were simpler solutions than the ones I had been trying to apply. By late morning, all the dishes, pots, and pans were back in their designated storage spots, and I headed in for the most peaceful sleep I had had in days.

When I awoke, it dawned on me that I had prepared more food than my small family could eat in a week's time. Not having enough refrigerator or freezer space either, I took it as an opportunity to invite some family and friends over to share the results of my therapy. My stress-reduction activity turned out to be a party. Having people around me and socializing was also beneficial to my previously down mood. Everyone was pleasant and appreciated the spur-of-the-moment invitation. Most of all, no one went home hungry.

Not that I'm recommending marathons, but baking and cooking can be very successful at relieving stress and its symptoms. In the amount of time it takes to bake a cake or prepare a meal, attitudes can be changed, burdens can seem less torturous, and your focus can be left much clearer.

There is something else I lean on no matter what is tampering with my mood. It's that wonderful invention called the telephone. Picking it up and dialing someone's number is one of the easiest tools to use when you need to manage. Airing the problem vocally stops me from holding it in and brooding over it. Talking it out with a friend lets me see things from someone else's point of view, which can be very different than my own. During the discussion, we can toss around solutions. If they don't come about, it's still a very reassuring feeling to know that another person is concerned and hoping the best for me. On the opposite, hearing of someone else's problems could bring to light that I am not as bad off as I believed to be.

I have a dear friend in Toronto, who I consider my soul sister, who I call upon when I need someone to hear me out. There is an unspoken understanding between us that it's a two-way street when it comes to needing support. She calls on me for help when she needs it as much as I call on her. Sometimes, we get these hunches about each other and have to make time to call the other as soon as we can. Several times our hunches have proven right, and the other did need an ear to bend or a shoulder for support. We are equally honest with each other and openly say what we feel. One thing I've learned through her about dealing with situations is being open to criticism. It may not always be others at the root of your problems. It may be something I do consciously or subconsciously. Regardless of where fault lies, we support each other and assure each other that better days will come.

A simple phone call can do wonders for cheering up that down mood. The same is to be said for e-mails and instant messaging. The knowledge alone of having someone to reach out to can be soothing to the nerves.

Along with simple meditations, past life regression is also something I have resorted to for answers and relief. I bought a CD that my friend at The Guardian in Cape May recommended. Even though I fell asleep the first few times I popped the CD in, I stuck it out. The key is to go into a deep meditative or hypnotic state, not sleep like a baby. About the fourth try, I got results and an answer to one of my questions. Have I overcome more in this lifetime than any previous ones?

My regression took me back to when I was a young geisha girl. I was approximately twelve years old. During my regression, I was wearing a traditional kimono and sitting in a garden on a stone bench with my older sister. Ironically, this older sister appeared to be Asian, but when I looked into her eyes, I could clearly see that she was my older sister of the present day. (They do say the eyes are the windows to one's soul.) Even though I didn't see it, I was well aware of what had taken place before we met in the garden. My sister was sent to talk and convince me that I was wrong in my thinking. I had been rebelling against being a geisha girl. I could feel so many emotions, as if they were in me right then. There were feelings of hatred, violation, sadness, loneliness, oppression, depression, anger, and more. My sister was telling me that I had to stop my silliness and accept the way of tradition and family. There was no other choice but to give in and accept this was to be my life. I held my chin high at her and let her know I could not live that life. We parted. She returned toward what I assume was our home. At the end of the garden path, I walked toward my right. Alongside of me was a row of shack-like buildings. They appeared to be people's homes. Beneath my feet, the path was laid with loose stones and pebbles. I passed chicken coops before coming to a clearing at the bottom of a small hill. In the clearing were crops, and beyond them was a wooded area. On top of the hill was another building. It seemed to be some sort of worker's shed or toolshed. I went in and carried something out in my hand. Back outside the shed, I looked out across the crops to the trees. The weight of all hope lost was embedded in me. I felt defeated and broken. The wetness of tears felt so real on my face. My regression ended soon after, but I knew I was headed toward the wooded area. I also knew and could feel the intensity of it all. I was going to kill myself. Rather than face a life that was dealt me, I chose death.

One might be asking how this answers my question or gives me relief from my present-day situations. As sad as living as a geisha girl would have been and how it ended, I have overcome and achieved more than that in this lifetime. In both lives, it is apparent to me that I have always had high morals. Another connection of the two lives is that both were tainted by me being violated under another's influence or control. Yet in the previous, I chose the easy way out. During my regression, I could tell I had a strong will to fight and rebel for what I believed. I did not stand up for myself. I ended my life and took the easier route out.

In this life, I also have that same strong will and sense of rebellion in me. The fact that I have persevered, seen things through, and come out the winner even stronger is a great feat. In many ways, I have made up for my past life and made up for the childhood lost in this one. Past mistakes have been corrected, and my soul has grown spiritually from it.

Yet another thing I have found that has a great impression on me mentally and physically is the amount of sleep I get each night. My sleep patterns result in how I feel in many aspects throughout each day. Night after night of minimal or disturbed sleep can be very damaging to my thinking and energy levels. I am drained physically and have little to no ambition. My thoughts become scrambled, out of focus, and lean toward the negative. It is of major significance that I go to bed at a reasonable time each night. I have had to learn to listen to my body physically. Not doing so brings down my mental state. My body and mind will scream out when I am lacking sleep. I have to acknowledge the urgent request and put all other things aside to get the proper rest I need.

Before my breakdown, it was extremely rare that I would rest or nap during the day. To settle down was near impossible for me. Today, I am the complete opposite. I am a master napper. I take that few minutes to an hour in the afternoons when I need it. It's not worth a good ounce of anything to push myself to the point of exhaustion. Whether I get the rest I need from a night's sleep or a nap, my body and mind are given the chance to shut down and reenergize. The times when I have suffered from insomnia were because I was not allowing my mind and body to turn off. These were the times that my mind raced uncontrollably and fed off what little physical strength I had. I walked around like a zombie by day and could not function anywhere near my normal capabilities.

Whatever the reason for being down, it is important to not hold it in. It is important to vent the frustration, anger, or grief. It's equally important to express joy and pride with the good feelings and events also. Journaling is a resource I, along with many others, resort to. Writing out good or bad feelings is a form of releasing both. Another way I do this is by going to my therapist. I still schedule regular monthly visits with her as a tool to keep reign over my daily life. She is my way of touching base and seeing where I've been and where I'm headed. She is the person who listens without judgment or discrimination. My forty-five minutes with her can be spent venting or reflecting. It all depends on what I need mentally.

When I tell people that I have or had an appointment with my therapist, I at times get a reaction that is biased and stereotypical. Some people tend to automatically assume that someone who sees a therapist or psychologist is a "psycho" or "nutjob." It makes the circumstances more awkward when people take an obvious step backing away from you. Hello. News flash, I'm not contagious. It can be irritating and aggravating that even today, with all that has been proven, people still think the same way people did decades ago. In the same sense, I feel pity for them because of their naivety and set-mindedness. My reaction to them is to enlighten them, as much as vindicate myself, with a simple statement that says I am a better person, for seeking help with my faults, than others who choose to brew in their issues and remain in a lifestyle that is unhealthy.

I have to learn to accept these uneducated types and accept them for their own faults. I also have to remind myself of their positive attributes to bring about that balance of acceptance. All of us have issues in our closets, and no one here on this earth is perfect. In no way am I ashamed that I suffer from depression here and there or that I went so far as to admit myself to a hospital for it. I don't go running to the mountaintops to announce it, but when appropriate, I will tell another about my experience. We all have things in our past. Hiding them only causes us to live behind those masks and rose-colored glasses. I fully accept that I am a sufferer of depression. It is my cross to bear in life, just as a diabetic has to accept his limits and symptoms of his or her illness. Similarly, a diabetic, like a depressive person, has skills and tools to cope through the down times and maintain the good ones.

It is wonderful to prove my own self wrong. I used to view myself as weak, dependent, and lacking in so many fields, I would have never imagined being the person I have become. I have the high confidence to say I am strong, courageous, independent, and loyal. I am worthy of the blessings I have been given as well as worked hard for. I am normal, like millions in the world who have struggles and down times. These are a standard part of growing in life. They do not in any way reflect that I am stupid or more deserving of them. I am certain that I am a fairly intelligent person, and overcoming obstacles is proof of my capability to persevere. That person who I once believed I was is far from my self-vision today and a distant memory.

I am often posed the questions: what regrets do I have in life, and what ones would I go back and change if I could? My answer today is a rather frank "none." My former self would have pondered the question before hesitantly answering, because I hadn't looked back at every little detail. Today I have none of those delays in supplying a reply. Each and every thing that has happened to me in life has impacted where I am today. Without them, I may not be as willing to grow or be as strong. Besides, on the mythical chance that we could go back and be granted do-overs, there is no guarantee that the thousands of different possible scenarios would make our lives better or easier.

This makes me think of Aesop and the words he's known to have spoken. "We would often be sorry if our wishes were gratified." No, thank you. I accept my past for what it is and what it has enabled me to do.

It's clear that I still work on myself today. But that is not the only thing I am busy with. Up until last year, my husband and I were still foster parents. It was something we stumbled into a few years ago, completely unprovoked and unintentionally. It was always very rewarding and challenging at the same time. To borrow the phrase from the US Army, I can best describe it as not just a job, but an adventure. People tended to think we are a bit crazy, and that could be true. However to be able to nurture and provide a child with healthy and safe surroundings is not a challenge everyone can accept. I was not working outside the home, so that enabled me the time to devote to these children. At that point in time, my job was to stay home and rear these children who desperately needed my services. By no means did we do it for the money. Pretty much what the agency subsidized to us went right back to food, clothing, activities, and necessities most months. Consumed many days by the needs of our foster children, I depended on those few hours each week spent alone by myself to attend astrology class.

When I am finished with this writing project, I intend to look into taking a course at our local college. Only in my midforties, it's still never too late to follow my dreams. Luckily for me, they have just built a campus within three miles of my home. I won't have to worry about a long drive at night or icy conditions in the winter months. First to check out is a creative writing course and then possibly a second language. I took Spanish way back in high school. I will most likely continue the study of it. No matter what field I end up in, having a second language is almost a necessity in today's world.

A long-awaited dream of mine recently came true. Our house is rather small but quaint. I have nicknamed it The Shoebox Inn. Due to space limitations, I have never had a real opportunity to have family come and sit around the table to share a meal. We've held our share of outdoor picnics, but I don't feel the same bond or wholeness as I do when a meal is shared together. I have always held hope that it would happen one day. My parents and my husband's are getting older. I had always hoped to have them over for a meal with us, and I was starting to fear that it may become too late. After twenty years in our home, we finally saved enough cash to be able to add on. It was no grand, elaborate addition, just a dining room, but I am thrilled that I finally had the chance to cook and have our families over for Easter dinner.

While I try to make my wishes for nonmaterial things, this was a material one that had a personal or spiritual purpose. Having a dining room meant so much more to me than space or increased monetary value to my home. After everyone left the first time I served Easter dinner, I could feel that wholeness I had been missing all those years waiting. My home, which is a reflection of me, at last had that missing piece. Gathered around the table were the family members who are dearest to my heart. In my opinion, having them here and feeding them was the ultimate symbol of expressing my love and gratitude. By them accepting our invitation, it showed me they feel the same toward me in return. I needed to open my home and share the blessings I have received: my husband, my children, my surroundings, and talents. I was able to show them their place in our hearts as well as their place around our table. Now I look toward the future holding many more opportunities to feed loved ones.

I can't say I've reached my full growing potential as of yet. That is a belief I will never sway from. I am still unveiling little things about myself that I didn't realize or understand before. We all learn or gain something each day that impacts who we are. To accept that we are done with the growing process, to me, is the equivalent of saying we're deceased. I also hold faith that we do not die until we have met all the challenges and purposes we are supposed to encounter in our lifetime. No one goes before his or her time here is done. I have no idea when my time will be finished here. I just accept that I am to go through certain things and to gain learning experiences in each of them.

What seems like eons ago, when I became involved with my daughters' school, I became aware of some moral and physical wrongdoing being committed by our pastor. He was someone with whom we had placed full trust and respect in. That trust was broken in many ways. There were proven financial issues concerning hidden and missing money that was donated to the school on behalf of my husband by his employer. Going to the pastor's superiors and sharing the knowledge and evidence in our possession was ignored and swept under the rug. Avoiding a lot of detail, the end result was what I would describe as spiritual rape. The religion I had been raised to believe in was suddenly marred by hypocrisy, greed, and deceit. I lost faith and trust in the people who were supposed to guide me spiritually. In my heart, I tried to look past this and remain faithful. I could not get past the hurt from the experience. I left the church and have not regained the trust to return.

I was baptized and raised as a Roman Catholic. Today I do not practice a set religion. Rather, I have a more personal relationship between my god and me. I stay connected with him through prayer, meditation, and my actions. Each night before going to bed, I give thanks for what the day has brought me. In the morning, I thank him again for granting me another day to try again. My bond with him is stronger than it ever was when living the rules set by the Church. I admire people who have that ability to worship and praise him through services and mass. I used to beat myself up because I could not find the strength to go to a designated building to pay homage. I've moved beyond that and accept that my faith has that limitation. For now I don't want to take the chance of other people or practices coming between us as it had in the past. Perhaps in time, I will be enlightened to a specific religion or place where I am meant to praise him. I remain open to the signs that will lead me there. In the meantime, I keep him close by and look for him in my surroundings, whether it is through loved ones, nature, or my thoughts and actions.

My relationship with my daughters has grown tremendously. There is an even blend of parent and friend. They approach me for advice when they need it. Otherwise, I keep that safe distance from judging and telling them how it should be like the experienced parent wants to do out of natural instinct. It is wonderful to see how they have spread their wings and flown. It brings pride to my heart to know I was one of the key players in developing who they have become. The pride can be overwhelming, causing a tear to come to my eye, because in reality they are a reflection of me in some aspects. I'm secure in saying I did a good job as a parent. I've had my great doubts in the past. It's interesting to see the paths they are following. I anxiously wait for them to make the next turn. These are the moments when I am so gracious for being here, overcoming my childhood experience, and pulling through the depression. Today, I am their number-one cheerleader, as well as the shoulder they need during a rough time.

Our oldest daughter graduated this year from college. She has earned her bachelor's and master's in accounting in just four years. She's not only brilliant, she's extremely independent. Out of the suburbs where we raised her, she loves living the big-city life.

Our youngest daughter graduated from high school and chose to lease her own apartment nearby. Working a full-time job and attending night school keeps her busy. She still suffers from her leg injury. Rarely does she have a pain-free day. Still, she has maintained a 4.0 grade point average. Both of our daughters have made us extremely proud. Of course, I will always count them as my special blessings.

My husband still remains my number-one support in life. He has had my back through thick and thin. I owe him much more credit than I have given him throughout these pages. It is not an easy thing to stick by and watch someone go through struggles as I have. He never once has abandoned me or placed me second in his life. I have always admired how he can let things just roll off his shoulders. When I am trying to overcome an obstacle, I look to him as an example of how easy it can be to get over. What has always amazed me about him is the fact that, with all that I have been through and the accomplishments I have achieved, he fails to be surprised at me. He has never seen me doing anything other than prevailing. He has total belief in me, my abilities, and my strengths. He will forever be my best friend, hero, and knight in shining armor. We're thinking down the road, into the not so distant future. Our twenty-fifth anniversary is just over a year away. Our plan is to renew our vows, no place other than on the beach in Cape May, near the ocean.

We always pondered about the things we would do together when both girls moved out. All the brainstorming in the world could never prepare a parent for empty nest syndrome. It is a sudden burst of change, renewal, calm, and excitement all at once. Having an empty nest has its good and bad aspects. For us, it is proof that we did our job of raising our kids to be responsible, independent, and secure in themselves. In addition, we are free to go and do as we please, when we please. On the other hand, for me personally, it can be lonely. My daughters were what defined me for so long, it is hard at times not to have them here in the same house. I do miss them, but remind myself that I have earned this time to do all the things I have delayed for years.

We always struggled to find time for just the two of us. An occasional movie, a meal, just sitting and having any type of conversation was important to us. Finding quality time between us was essential to our relationship. While raising our girls, our relationship took on more of a business partner spin. Of course, our love for each other was still there, but it was not always most visible. Our kids were the obvious priority. Now we are enjoying rekindling the romance and spontaneity that we shared pre-parenthood. Ironically, we realize it's important to have time alone, without the other, once in a while. Keeping our individuality is one of the main reasons we've been together for all these years. It's fascinating to see how we have grown together. Our bond together is stronger than ever. Many things are the cause of our strength. Maturity, experience, respect, and our spirituality all play a role. Sincerely, I know I am able to love more deeply today because I have released all of the negativity and obstacles that existed in my life when we started dating twenty-six years ago. Being completely healed from being molested, I am free to put 100 percent of my mind, body, and soul into our relationship.

Although they are up in years, my parents still live in the house my father built. I am fortunate to still have them both. While I was growing up, neither of them ever spoke of love. They gave my siblings and me the best they could. I understand now this is how they expressed their love for all seven of us. When I was in the mental facility, my mom called to talk to me. For the first time, she said, "I Love You."

I reciprocated the same words with tears in my eyes. Hearing these words was something I craved and needed as a child. The times she has said it since still bring pure joy to my heart like that first time. In a way, those three small words made up for much of the nurturing that was missing from my childhood. Even though they didn't come until I was an adult, they are still treasured just the same.

Today, in regards to the relationships I have with my brothers, I can say neutrally that they exist. No ill feelings linger or have developed in the near-eighteen years since our meeting. On the other hand, we never developed any type of bond beyond siblings by blood. We see each other at family functions. Being that all of our children are grown, there are fewer events. We do the normal catching up on how things have been and what is new or different. There will always be concern for each other and respect of parents being the bond that holds us together. I feel it fair to say it may never go further than that. In truth, what deters us from advancing in our relationships is the difference of personalities and lifestyles. Clearly, I am a female, and they are males. My interests lie in my daughters, the metaphysical, trips to the beach, and crafts. Their interests involve their sons, sports, and the woods and forest, where they hunt and fish. How we have raised our children varies considerably amongst all of us. I am a homemaker, housewife, domestic goddess, or full-time domestic volunteer, as I like to call myself. Their lines of work have led them to be construction workers, installers, engineers, and architects. Some of their jobs have entailed highly held positions within their companies. They look forward to slinging back a few beers now and again, while I can't get past the smell of it. It's sad to say we have little in common.

That is the reality that keeps a distance between us. Everything I've stated above about my brothers applies to my other two brothers who did not molest me. I don't have exceptionally close relationships with them either. We accept one another for all of the above differences, plus ones I didn't even make mention of. Our relationships could have turned out to be completely different than what they are today. We could have ones where there is never contact, no exchange of any conversation, or getting together ever. We still have the connection and respect of family. If I was ever in a situation where I truly and desperately needed their help, I don't doubt they would step forward to do what they could. The same would apply if they were in a bad situation. We all hope for the best and wish for nothing other than happiness for each other.

Although I am a well-recovered survivor, I still have my "aha moments" of insight regarding my past. Just recently, I had one of these clarifying flashes. Subscribing to Facebook was a way for me to communicate with my dearest friend and soul sister in Toronto. Being so far apart, posting photos and status updates brings us closer together.

To my surprise, classmates from high school started requesting to be my friend online.

Though a bit skeptical, I would confirm the request. Some have gone further to send an e-mail. To my astonishment, they all wonder where I got to and how is life going for me.

My high school days were not pleasant for me. Impacted by my molestation, I walked around in a fog, never realizing what was really going on around me. I recall having classes with these women and an occasional brief conversation with some of them. For them to search me out and take interest in my present life has caused me to realize just how way off my analysis of people was back in the day.

I am the one who put up the great wall of distance, a natural defense mechanism. No one other than my brothers had hurt me; I should not have feared anyone else. But the opposite was true; I trusted no one's motives. I never felt like I belonged or fit in with my classmates. It felt as though I appeared to every other being as having this dark glow of guilt and evil around my entire body that triggered people to be repelled by me.

Being part of the popular crowd was definitely not where I excelled. To have someone from that group make the first approach now reveals much to me. They were being friendly and reaching out to me with honesty those rare times I had spoken to them in high school. These girls were not being mean girls from the in-crowd as movies and TV stereotype them to be. I extend my sincerest apologies for thinking wrongly of so many.

Having them wonder why I never kept contact or went to our reunions shows me a lot that I missed and lost. Wishing that just one time I had reached back to any one of these girls will not change facts. We cannot go back in time and change things. I have to accept that there was no connection of feeling as if I belonged or bond of friendship.

This is how things were meant to turn out. In my soul, I believe at that time I was to have my mind consumed by the molestation. If I didn't and was preoccupied by friendships and school activities, I probably would have missed many of the insights I had that forwarded me in my recovery. As much as I despise thinking "what-if's," I'd have to say in this case, if my high school experience had been a more positive one, I would not be who or where I am at today. Conquering my molestation could well have been delayed or never happened.

So even today, my molestation still has a strong impact on my growth as an individual. Without any ounce of doubt, it will continue to do so in the future, but only in positive ways.

I can only learn more about myself and take pride in myself for sacrificing so much to have freedom from the guilt, torment, and destruction that being a victim brings to one's soul.

Overall, I am content and very happy with my life and how it treats me. I asked for support and time to work on my writing and was given it unconditionally by my family. I am very fortunate because most people don't get the chance to devote time to their goals as I have. I'm not out chasing rainbows. I'm busy watching the ones already around me. My wings are spread, and although I may not be soaring off on wild adventures, I am satisfied to be fluttering freely in my own direction. Counting my blessings rather than the notes on my resume or coins in my wallet keeps me feeling appreciative that I am here.

I can compare my whole life to a song by one of my favorite rock groups. The group being the well-known Aerosmith and their song titled "Amazing." The lyrics they sing sum up where I have been and where I stand at present. Truly listening to the words, I can place myself as the one who was going insane and dealing and walking through the pain. I could be the one who hit the floor and hoped to die. It's amazing, I could be the one who in the blink of an eye saw the light. I have seen when that moment arrives. You just know it's all going to be all right. I am definitely the one who prays for other desperate hearts regularly.

Surely this song was not written about me. I can guarantee you, even though it would be an awesome experience, I have never met any member of Aerosmith, nor do they know me. Maybe my thinking is completely different from what the words really mean. This is simply how I relate to the song and how I feel it connects to my life and me.

My one last wish that I would like to share is for every person on this earth to have the spontaneous, jaw-dropping moment in their life where you realize you are going to get through and you are exactly where you should be in life. The moment when you understand you haven't been on an awkward path, struggling for no purpose. To have such an epiphany of validation and personal truth strike you is an incredible feeling. There is no human being who does not deserve that colossal moment when they become fully aware that they have arrived. I have achieved it, and it is amazing.

On the first page, I shared the quote: "Everyone's story begins at home." My story certainly did. The middle of mine tells of how I overcame obstacles and burdens to find myself. It tells of how I was hidden beneath a mask of negativity and how I unveiled my soul to reveal my true self. The end has not been written yet. There are so many grand finales to choose from. Which direction and which turns of my plot come about will ultimately be my choice. I have the power and the control within in me to make my life happen as I wish. There is no doubt there will be obstacles for me to hurdle over along the road to the end. I do not fear them. I accept the challenges and lessons to be learned, for this is how my soul will continue to grow.

CHAPTER 13

Other Tips: Surviving on Your Own Island

Even skimming through the previous chapters, it is apparent that I have been motivated by inspirational quotes. Reading and repeating motivational quotes to myself gave me the nudge to think and, in some cases, to take action. Many of them have aided the change in my thinking. At times, reading a quote can bring attention to something I had not considered before. Often, upon reading one, I had to chuckle because it pointed out the obvious to me. A few simple words forming a sentence can bring to light the notion that brings me to understand or accept a situation. Quotes have been a tool that has brought about my insight and foresight. The numbers of times are countless that they gave me the little boost I needed to get through a rough day.

When battling the causes of being molested and my acute bout with depression, I constantly felt as if I was on a desolate island isolated from the rest of the world. Although I had others around me, I still had the sense of being alone in my dilemma. While it is important to have others nearby for support and comfort, I had to essentially work through all the issues on my own. No one could cure my wounds and make it all better but me. Therefore, in a sense, I was on my own island, and it took my willpower and applying any method I could to survive. If any one of us were literally deserted on an island, it would give us time to think. That's what reading quotes is for me. They give me time to think. The key to them having any type of impact is to read them with an open mind. One may just be the ticket to start your journey home from the island.

The following pages are a collection of additional thoughts, quotes, and self-advice that I have referred to in addition to the various coping mechanisms I have noted in my previous chapters. I have developed the habit of jotting them down in my journal or typing them into a saved document on my computer for future reference. Writing them down also helps me remember them later. They have all proved beneficial to me or made some impact that brought about a more positive attitude toward my circumstances. My hope for having this final chapter is one more chance of someone reading my words or another's and realizing that their own life can change for the better.

In the first section, I list many quotes by famous people. I have noted the person responsible for their quote. In the second section, there is no acknowledgement after. These are my views and thoughts that have come to me while on my journey. Rather than a bunch of wordy paragraphs with views on each, I will leave it up to the individual to reflect and draw their own conclusions. Here's hoping you, the reader, gets the boost you need to have a good day.

Section I

- "Oh, my friend, it's not what they take away from you that counts. It's what you do with what you have left." *Hubert Humphrey*
- "Life isn't about finding yourself. Life is about creating yourself." *George Bernard Shaw*
- "Change your thoughts, and you change your world." *Norman Vincent Peale*
- "Attitude is a little thing that makes a big difference." *Winston Churchill*
- "There are some defeats more triumphant than victories." *Michel de Montaigne*
- "Why not go out on a limb? Isn't that where the fruit is?" *Frank Scully*
- "When you're finished changing, you're finished." *Benjamin Franklin*
- "Turn your face to the sun, and the shadows fall behind you." *Maori proverb*
- "Life is a promise; fulfill it." *Mother Teresa*
- "A positive attitude may not solve all your problems, but it will annoy enough people to make it worth the effort." *Herm Albright*
- "If you find a path with no obstacles, it probably doesn't lead to anywhere." *Frank A. Clark*
- "When life's problems seem overwhelming, look around and see what other people are coping with. You may consider yourself fortunate." *Ann Landers*
- "Fear knocked on the door. No one was there when Faith answered it." *Old English proverb*
- "In the middle of difficulty lies opportunity." *Albert Einstein*
- "I am not afraid of storms, for I am learning how to sail my ship." *Helen Keller*
- "If you're going through hell, keep going." *Winston Churchill*
- "Learn how to be happy with what you have while you pursue all that you want." *Jim Rohn*
- "Faith is knowing there is an ocean because you have seen a brook." *William Arthur Ward*

- "If you don't run your own life, somebody else will." *John Atkinson*
- "The man who removes a mountain begins by carrying away small stones." *Chinese proverb*
- "If you haven't the strength to impose your own terms upon life, you must accept the terms it offers you." *T. S. Eliot*

Section II

- Tongue exercise. Talk, Talk, and talk. The more you do it, the more the pain eases.
- Listen with open ears as well as mind. Not doing so will block out the words that could prevent you from hearing the words you've been waiting to hear.
- Don't give up hope. Your intentions and dreams are always possible. When one tactic or approach doesn't work, try another. The finish line will eventually come into view.
- The easy part is setting a goal. The tough part is envisioning it and sticking with it to the end.
- Simplify! Get rid of any excess baggage that has no real or positive purpose in your life.
- Don't forget to toot your own horn. If you don't give yourself credit for even the tiniest achievement you make, how can you expect others to notice the work you've done?
- It is perfectly okay to talk to yourself out loud. You may just hear the advice you need somewhere in the conversation.
- Do not let others' opinions sway your own if you know better from experience. I have found it common practice for people to speak on subjects they have no experience with but express their views as having firsthand knowledge.
- You never know what will enlighten you and encourage you to keep fighting. I have been inspired by the teensy weensy spider from the popular children's' song. As many times as he tries to get up the spout, the rain knocks him down again. With some patience, the sun always comes up and dries up the rain. Once again, the spider goes back to aiming for the top of the spout. Oddly, I have compared my battle with depression to this determined and courageous spider.
- Keep your eyes open for opportunities. Being blind to them and fearing them will only keep you from the opportunity of change that could be the one that brings you true happiness.

- When you are sick and tired of hearing the same advice over and over again, perhaps you should make an attempt at using it. If it doesn't help, at least you have the satisfaction of hushing people when they nag.
- Always aim each morning to be a better person than you were the day before. It does not matter if it takes a week of days or years of them, as long as you become the person you wish to be.

The Beginning

(Not the End)

The Serenity Prayer

God grant me the serenity
to accept the things I cannot change;
courage to change the things I can;
and wisdom to know the difference.
Living one day at a time;
Enjoying one moment at a time;
Accepting hardships as the pathway to peace;
Taking, as He did, this sinful world
as it is, not as I would have it;
Trusting that He will make all things right
if I surrender to His Will;
That I may be reasonably happy in this life
and supremely happy with Him
Forever in the next.
Amen.

—Reinhold Niebuhr, expanded by William Spence in 1953